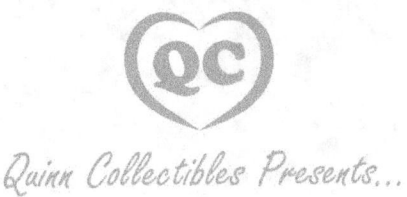

Quinn Collectibles Presents...

# SCI-FI BABES
## A Cyber Glam Coloring Book

By Stephanie A. Quinn

# SCRIBBLE AWAY!

**Use this page to test your colors!**

# Mira Mercury

Age: 28 Earth Years
Location: Currently lives on a spaceship.
She loves watching TV!

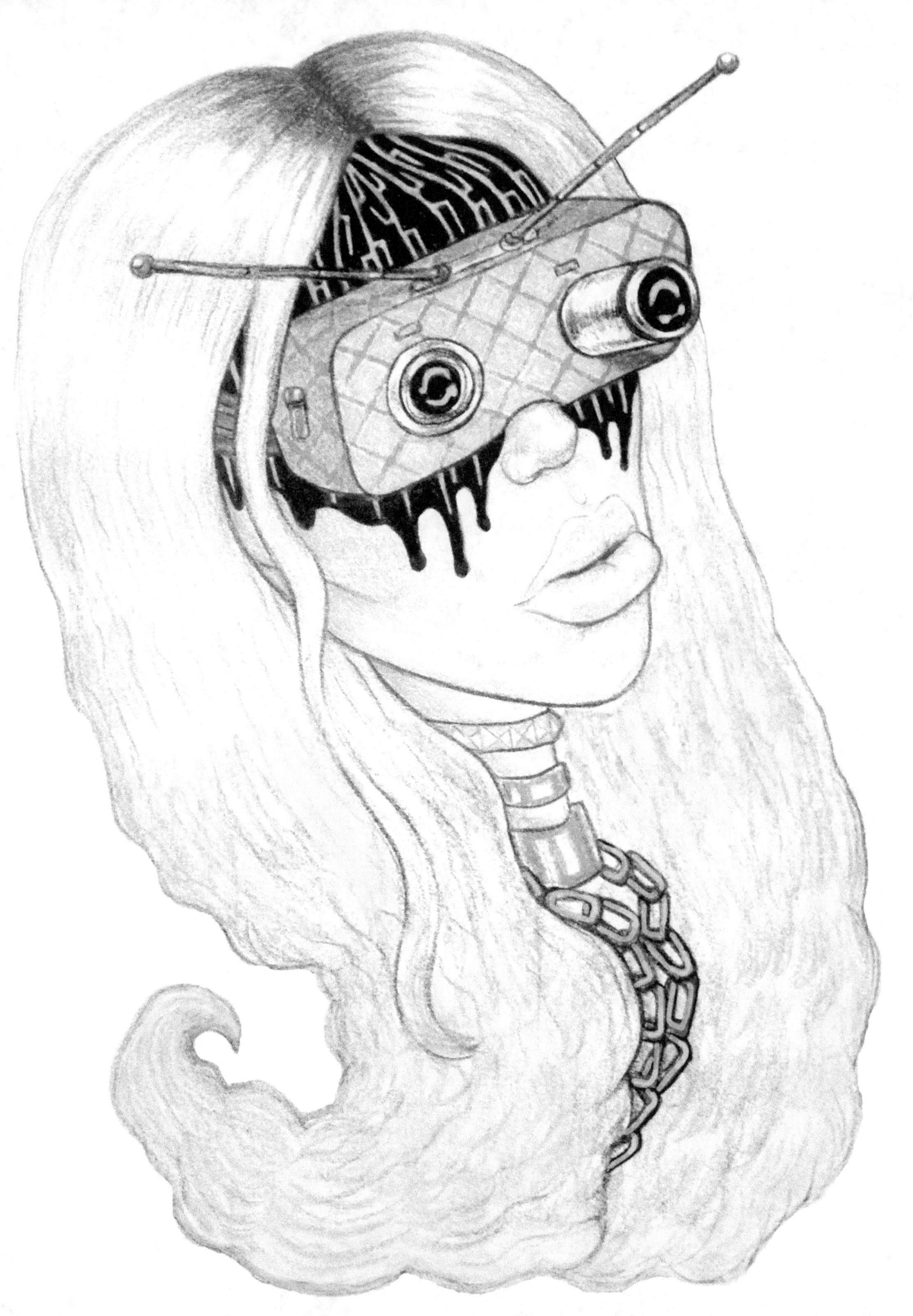

# *"Gamble"*

Age: 18 Earth Years
Location: Currently awaiting trial in intergalactic
court for candy theft.
She speaks ten languages.

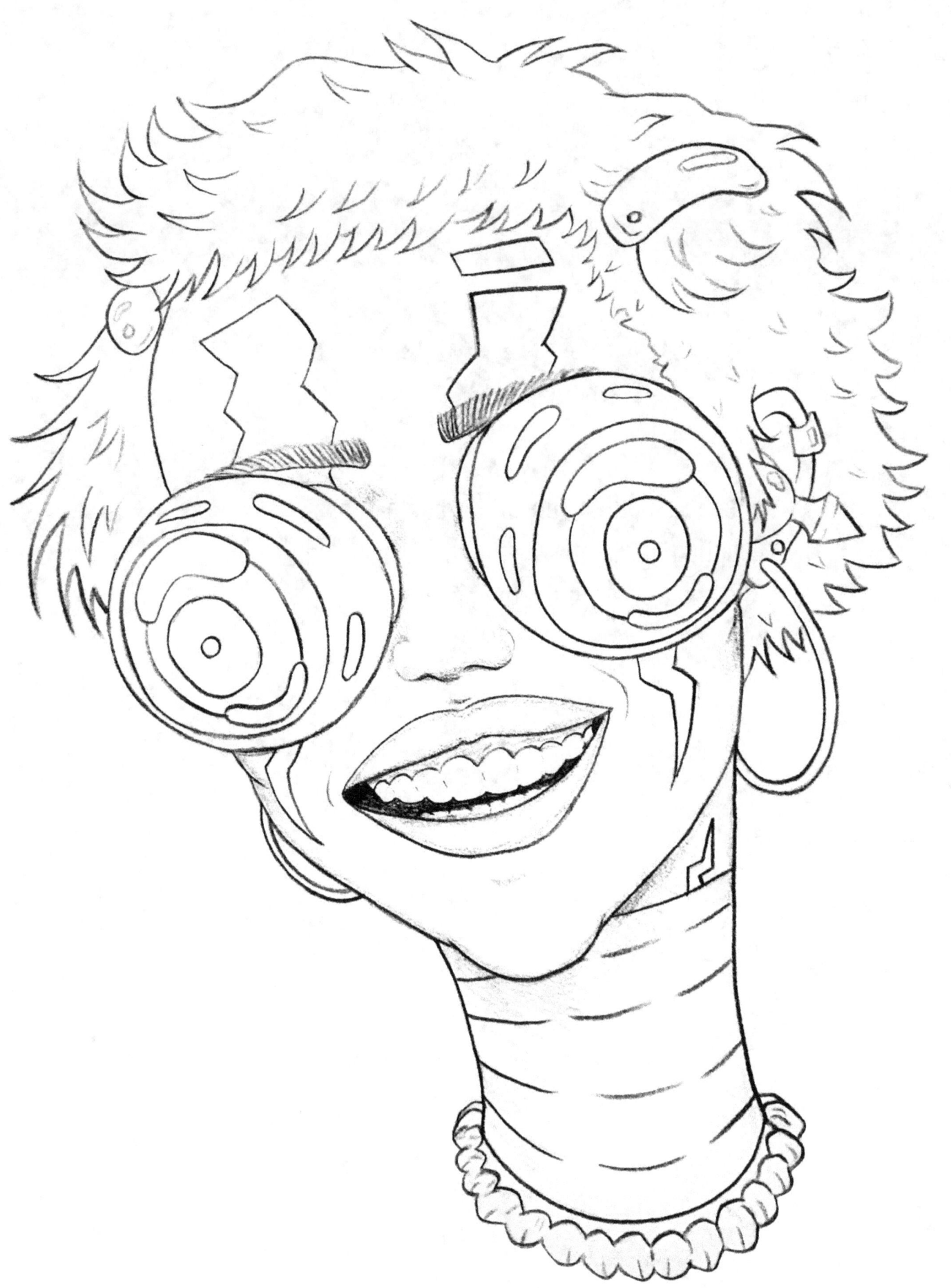

# Rachel Robot

Age: 3 Computer Years/ 33 Earth Years
Location: Currently lives in the World Wide Web.
She has a really good memory!

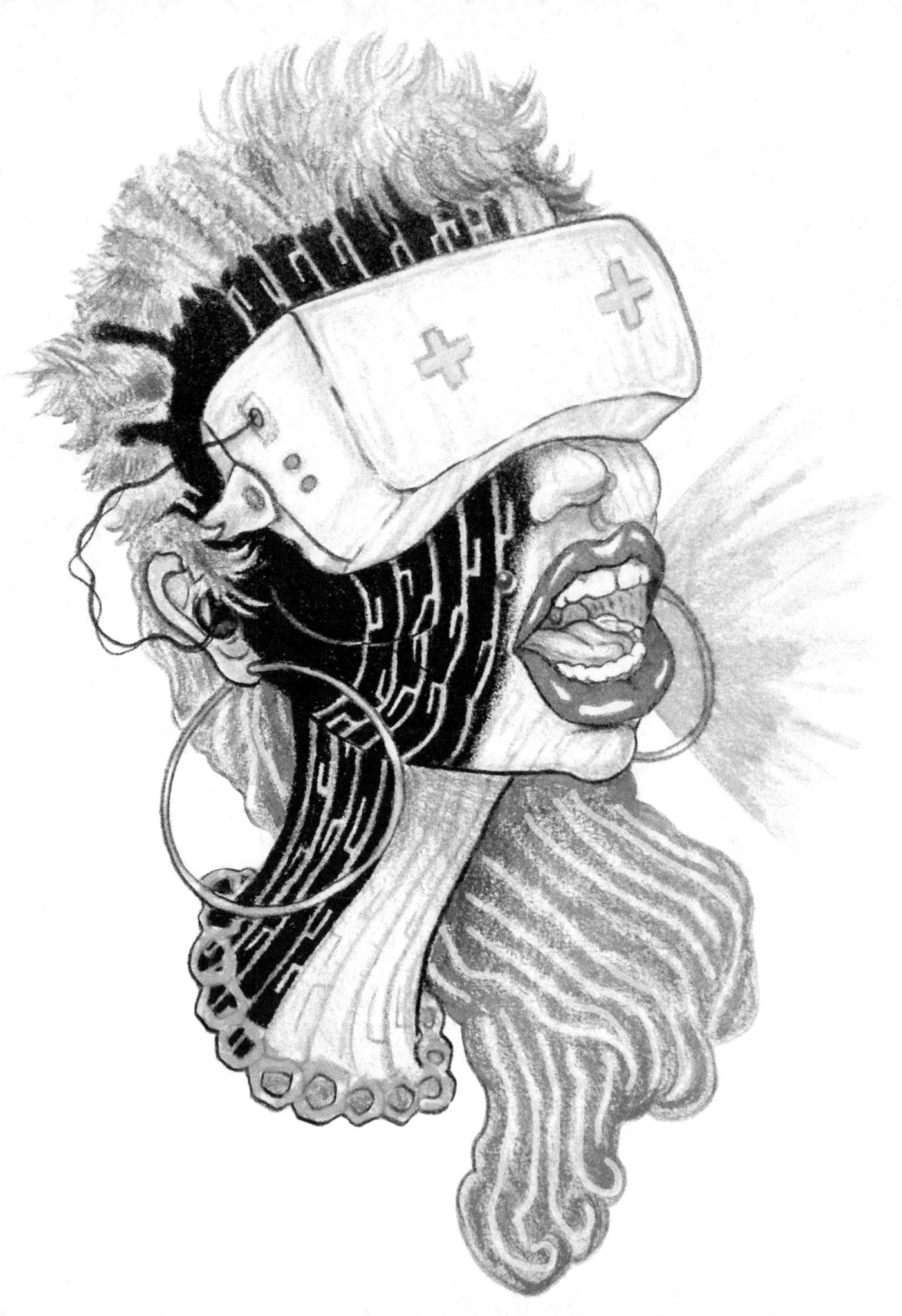

# Sally Space

Age: 32 Earth Years
Location: Voluntarily living out of her space car.
She is Rachel Robot's sister.

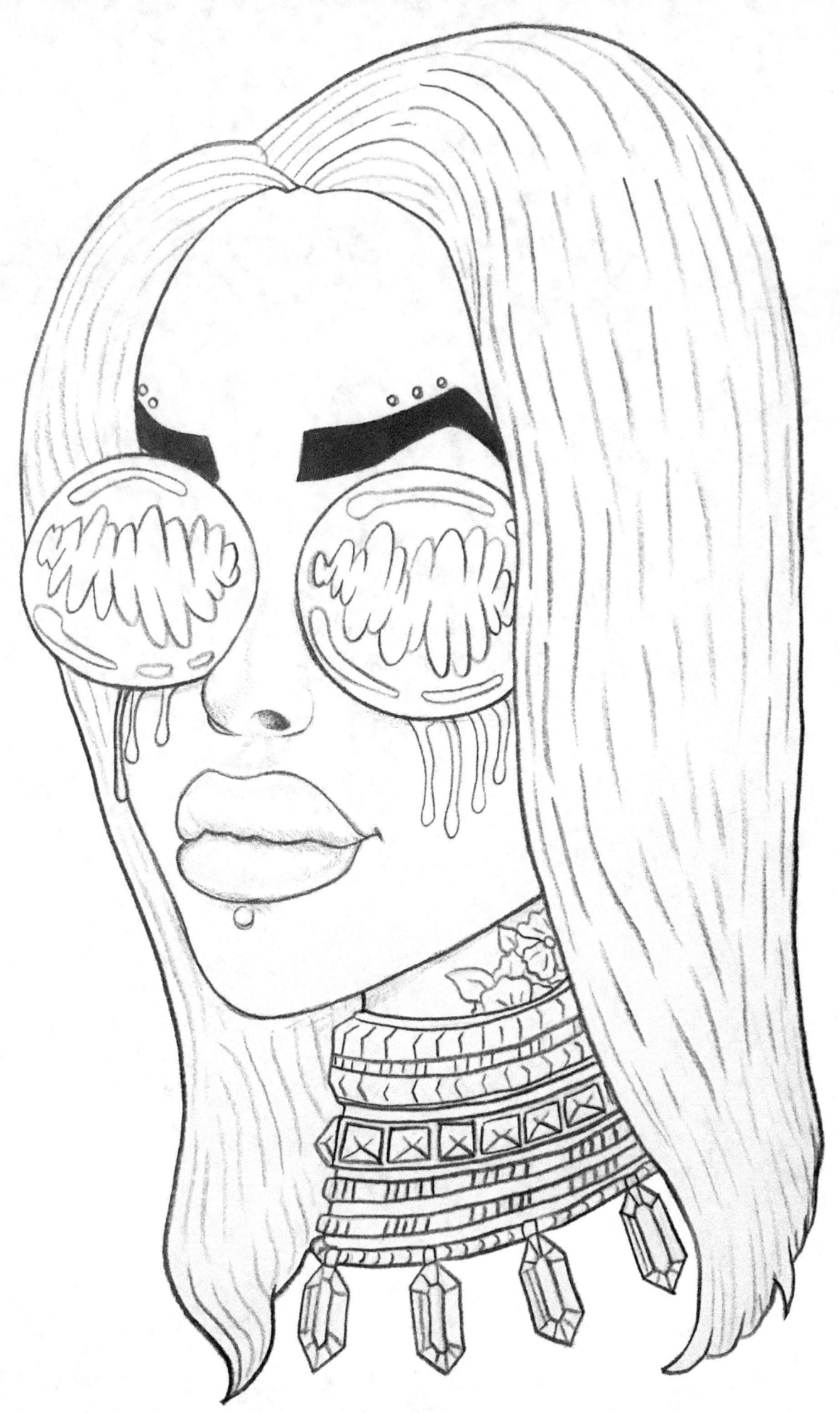

# Mistress Macroscope

Age: 173 Space Years
Location: Currently lives in a black hole.
She tries to see the whole world, just to grab it!

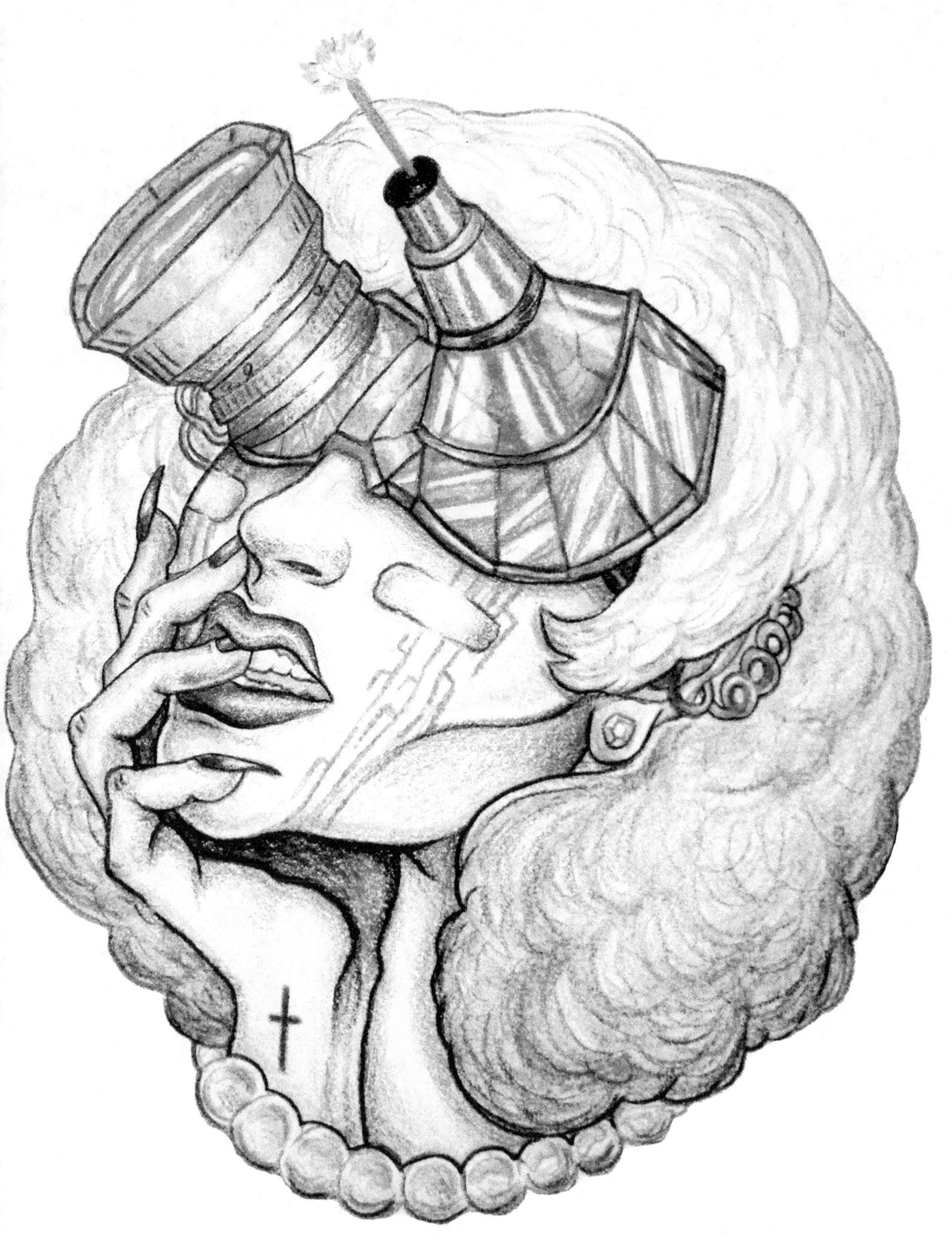

# Officer Laserbeam

Age: 29 Earth Years
Location: Currently on patrol under the Asteroid
Belt Police HQ.
She is an official Officer of Space.

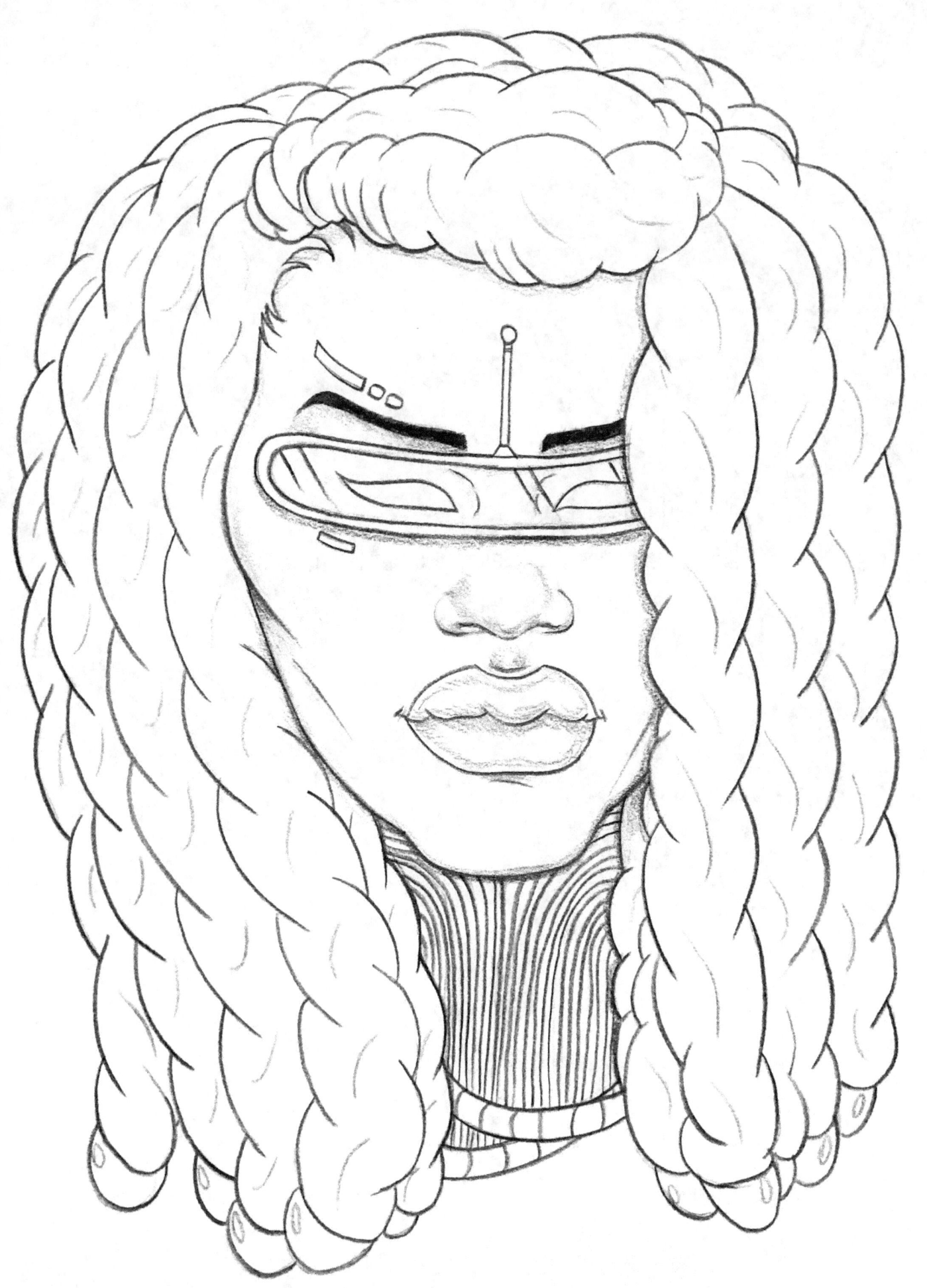

# Sheryl Scream

Age: 30 Earth Years
Location: Currently lives on Planet Earth.
She loves brain massages!

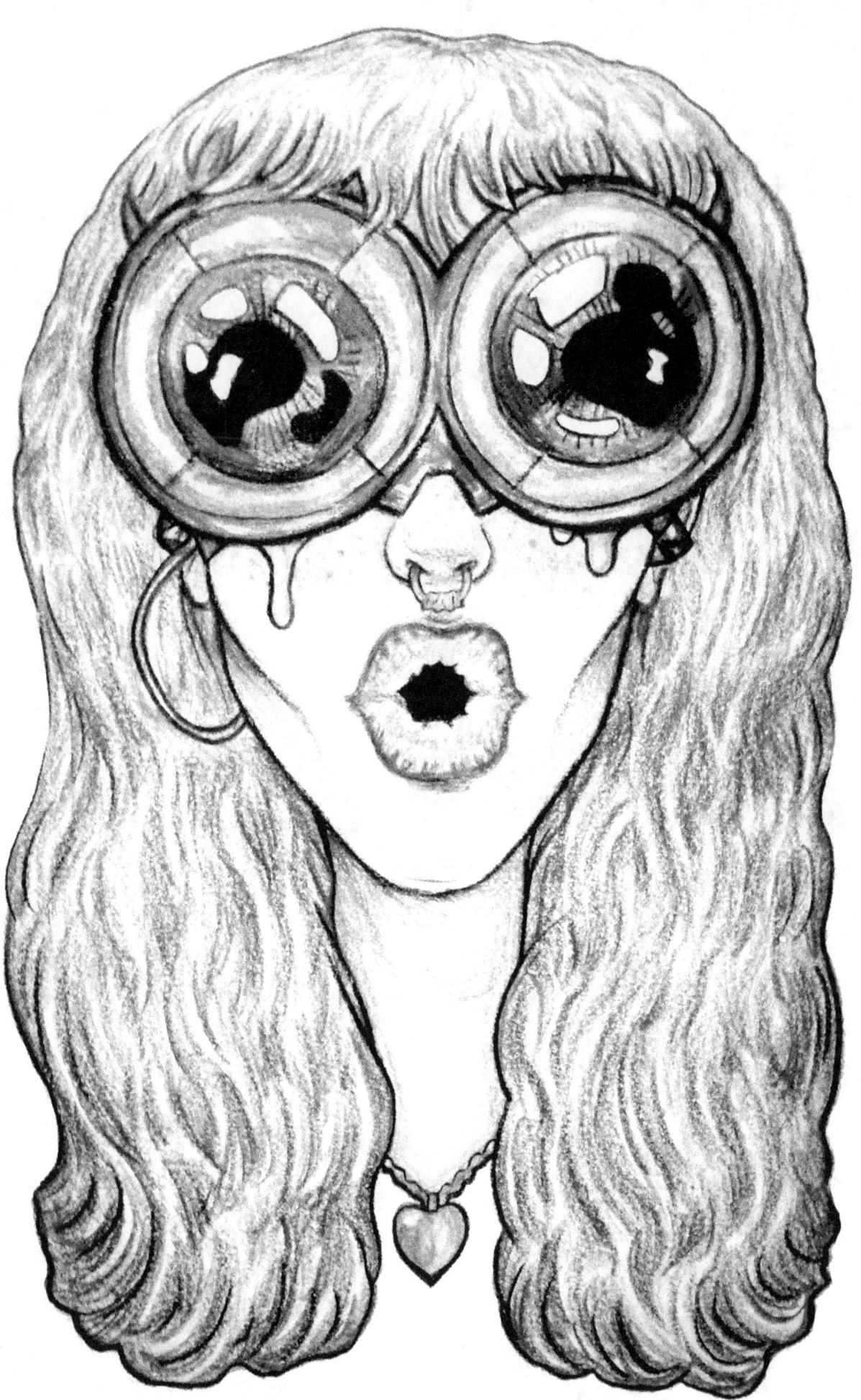

# Kelly Kosmos

Age: 21 Earth Years
Location: Currently living inside the moon.
She loves electronic music!

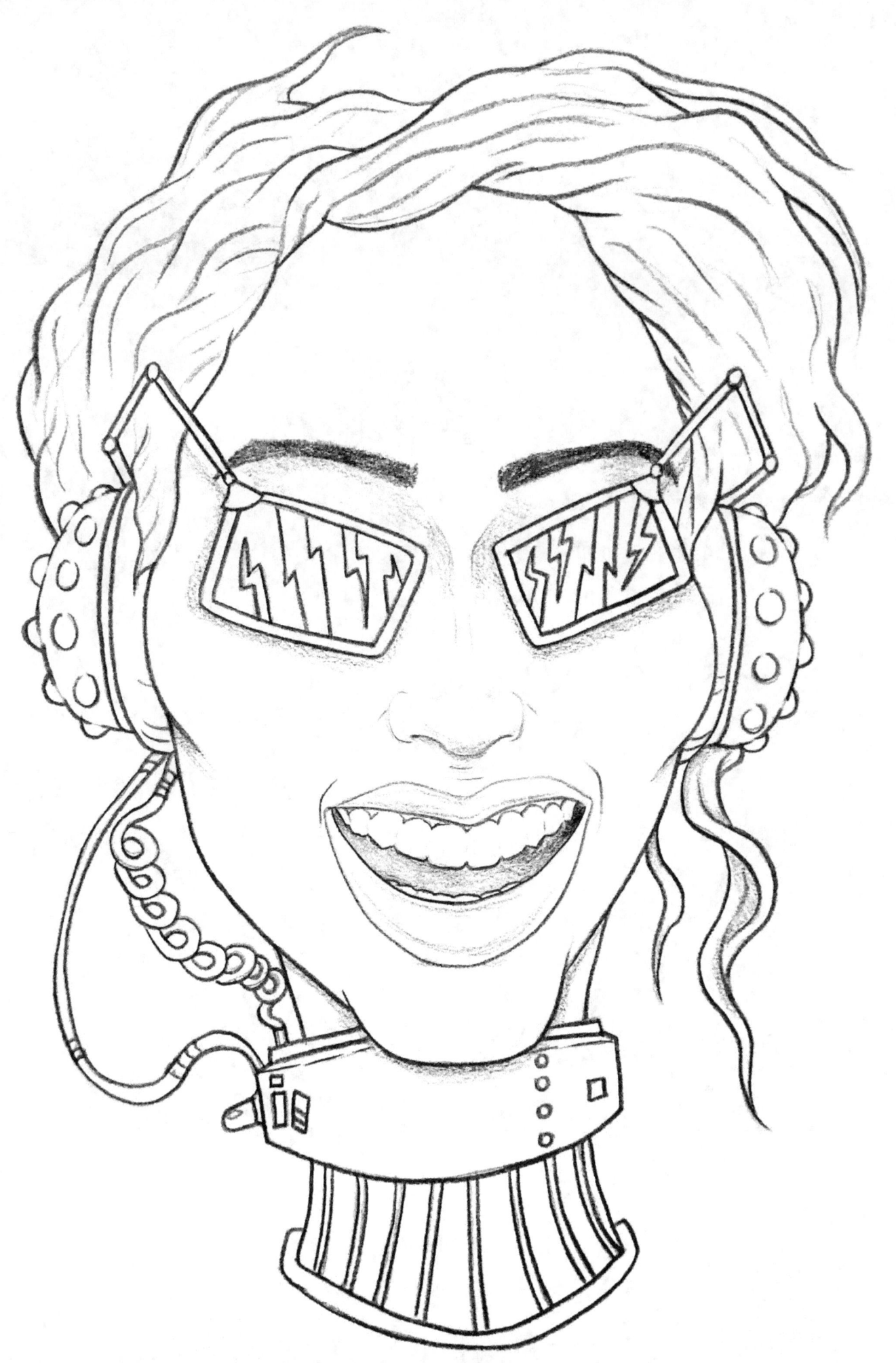

# Tiana Tenticle

Age: 125 Space Years
Location: Currently lives on an unnamed water
planet.
She is immortal, but was born recently.

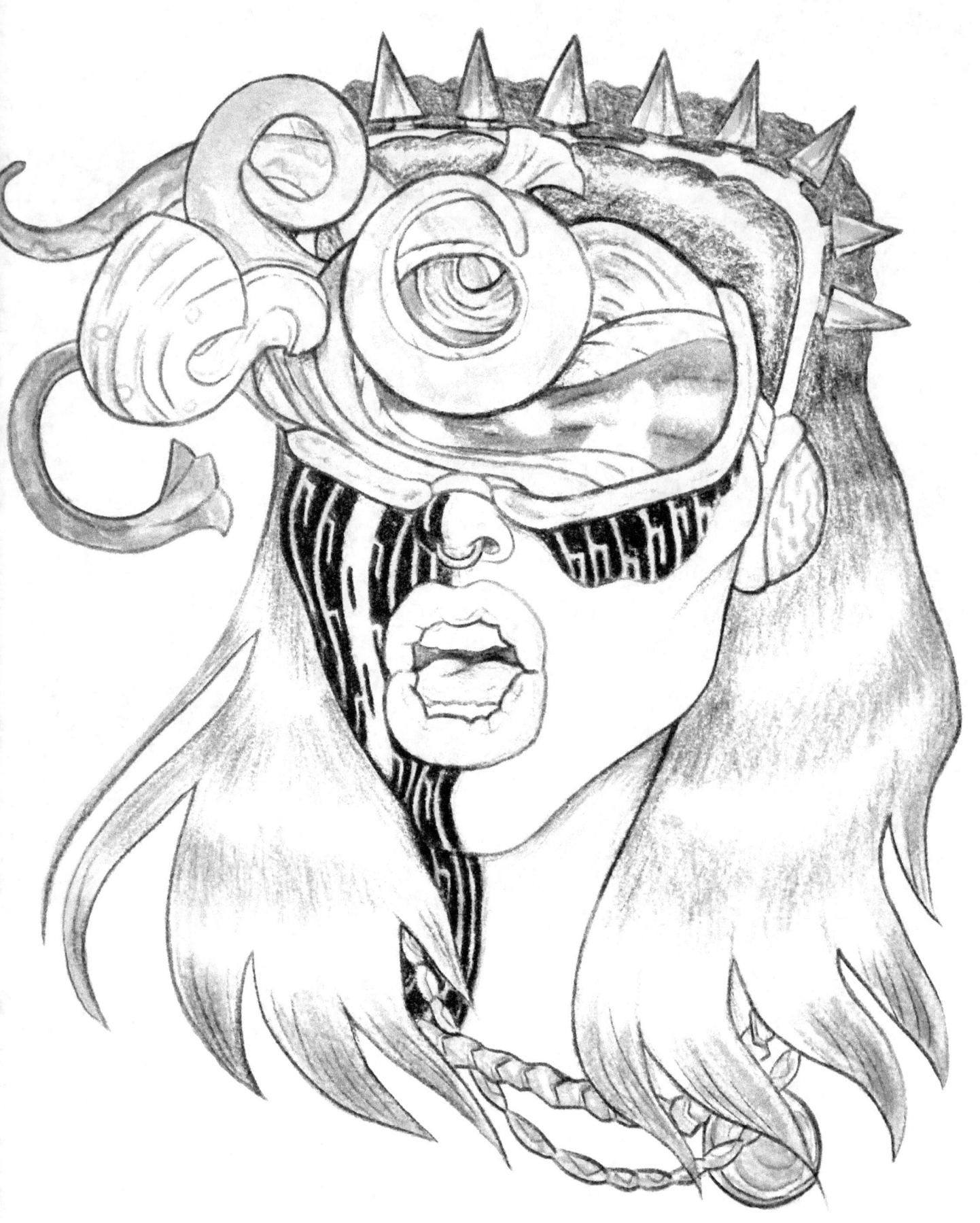

# Kitty Midnight

Age: 18 Earth Years
Location: Currently lives on a planet solely
inhabited by cats.
She doesn't know how she got there!

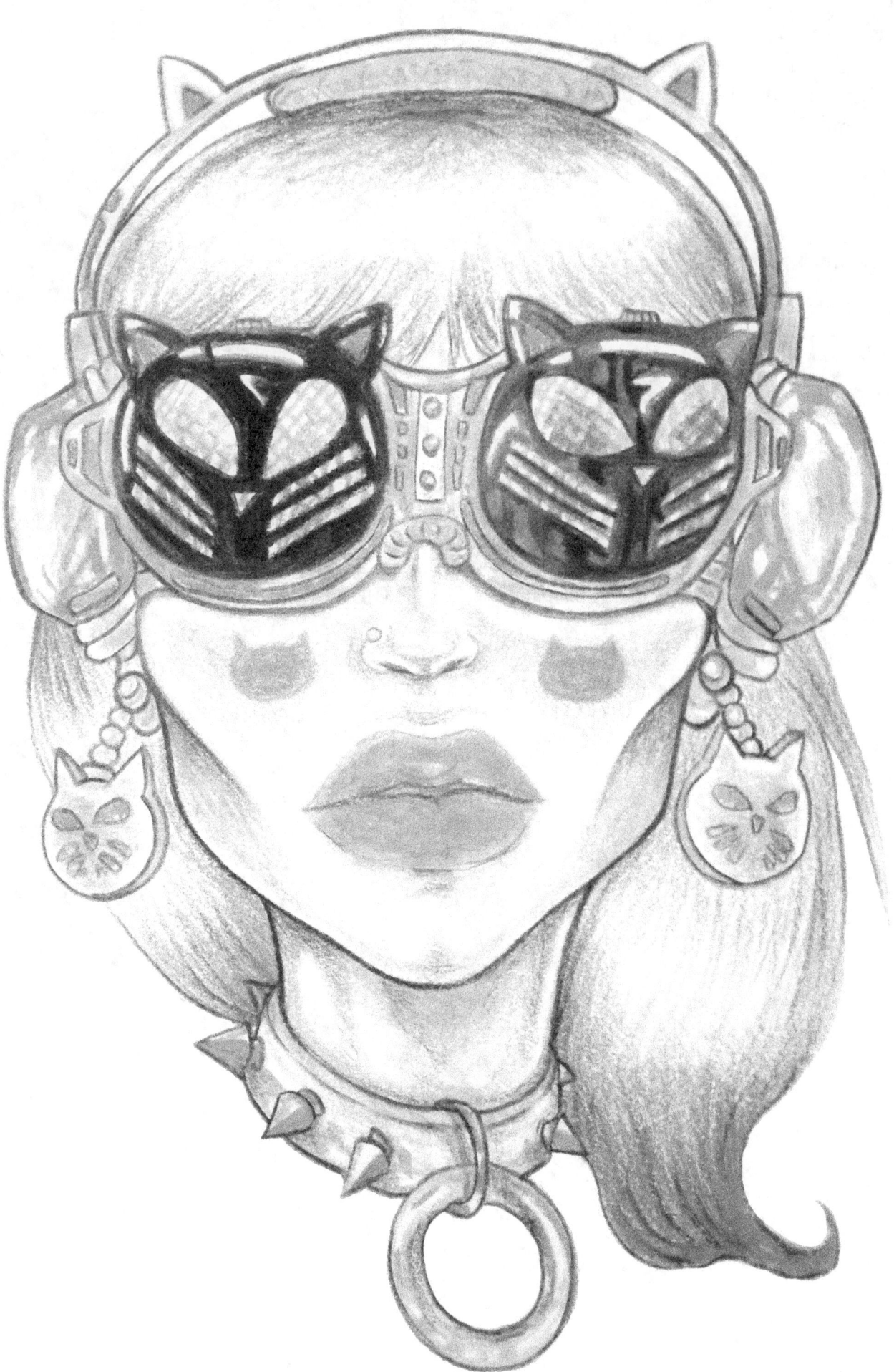

# Harmony Heart

Age: 26 Earth Years
Location: Currently on tour in the Alpha Centauri system.
She is a famous space performer.

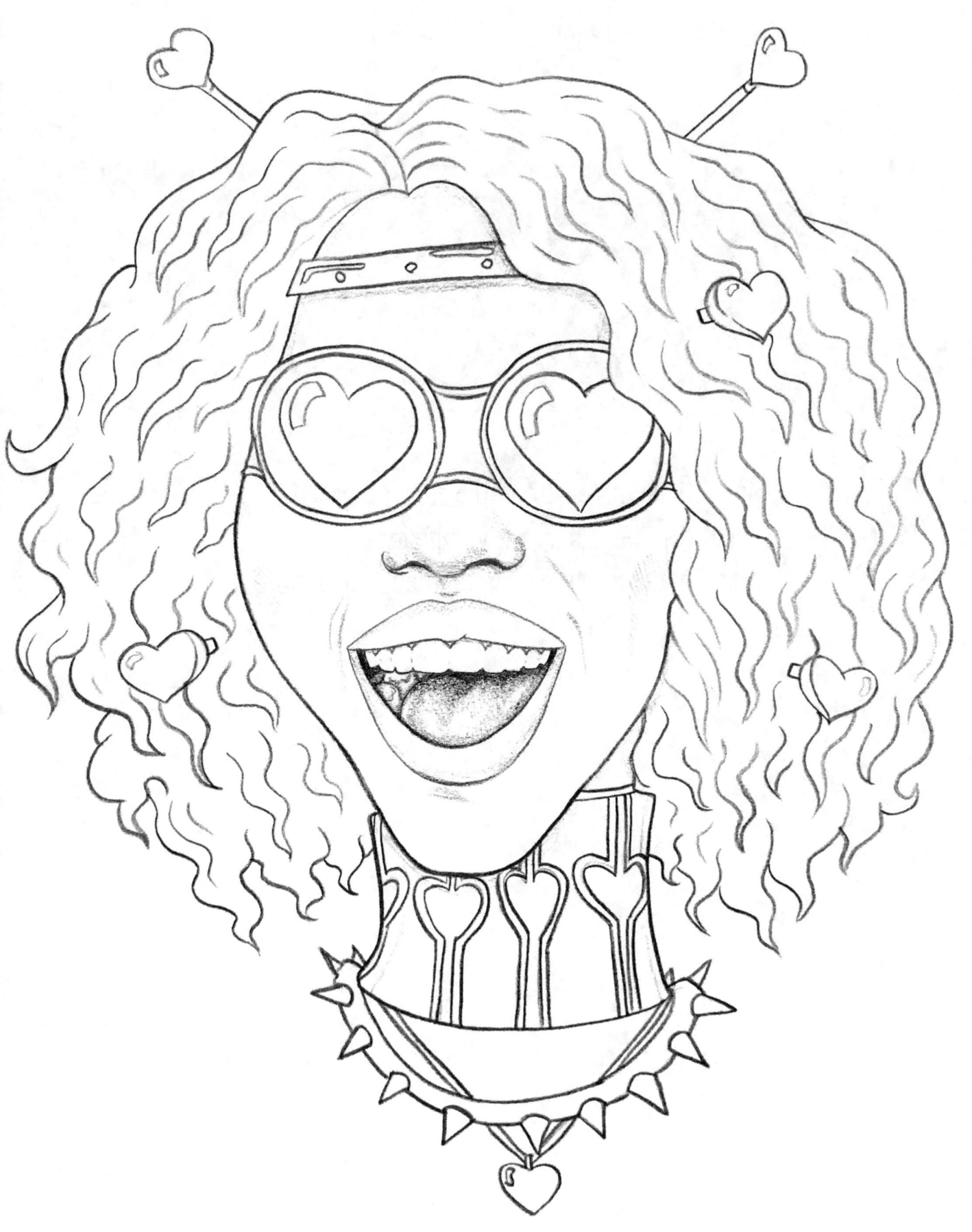

# Olga Orion

Age: 35 Earth Years/ 450 Robot Years
Location: She is currently in hiding.
She started off as a robot and became a human.

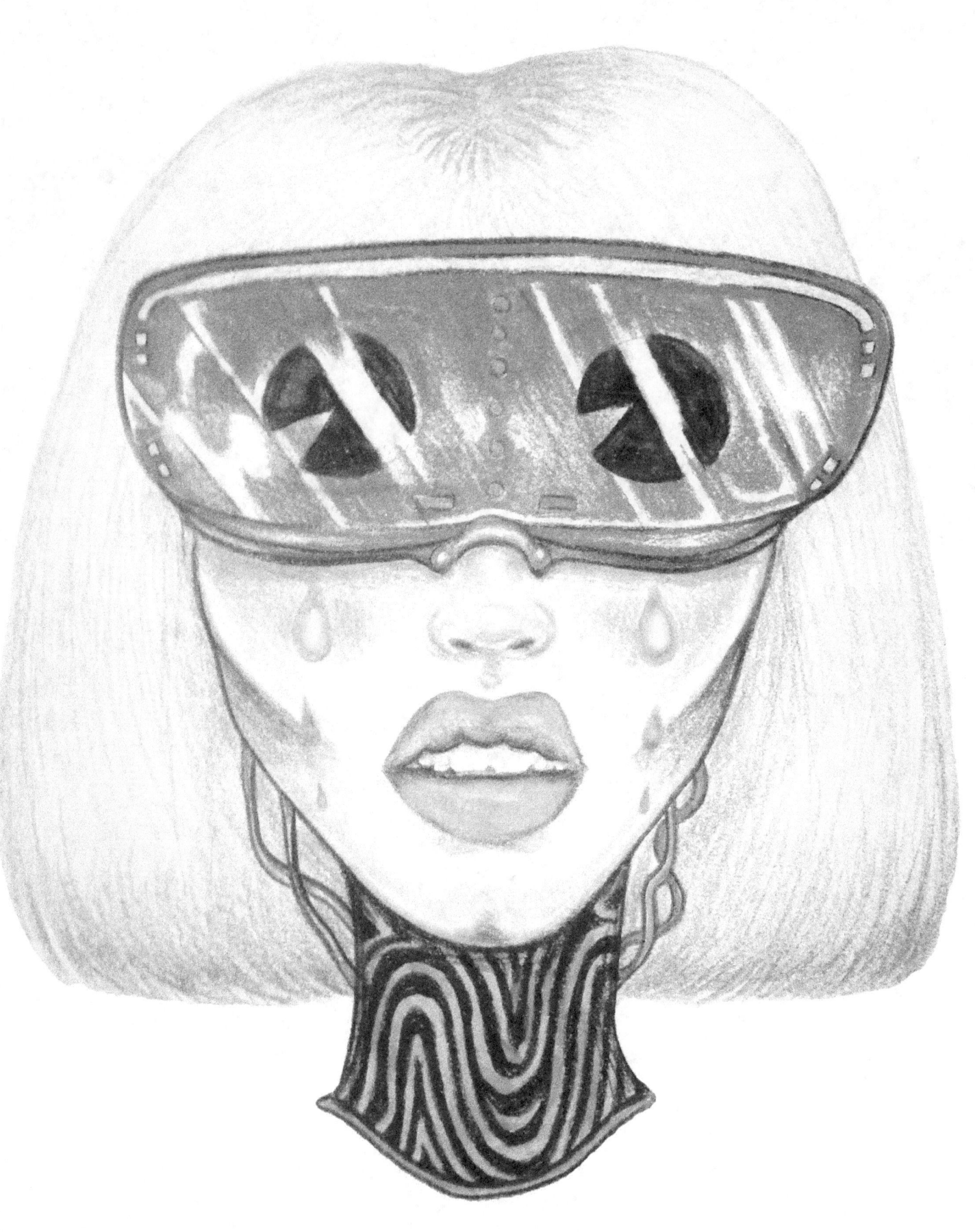

# Patti Planet

Age: 29 Earth Years
Location: Currently lives on Planet Earth.
She is an optimist!

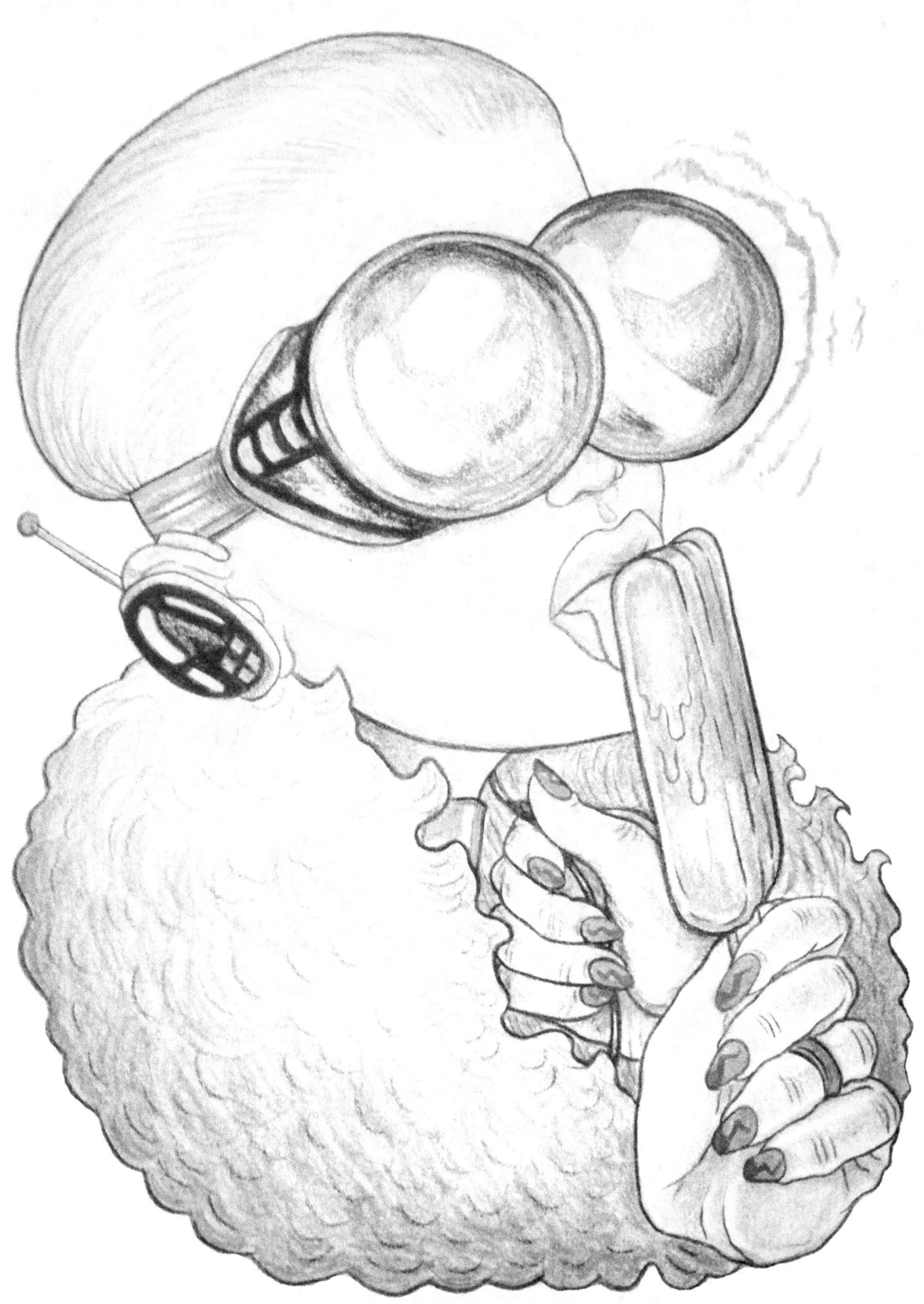

# Amy Asteroid

Age: 17 Earth Years
Location: Currently in math class.
Her ears are really cold!

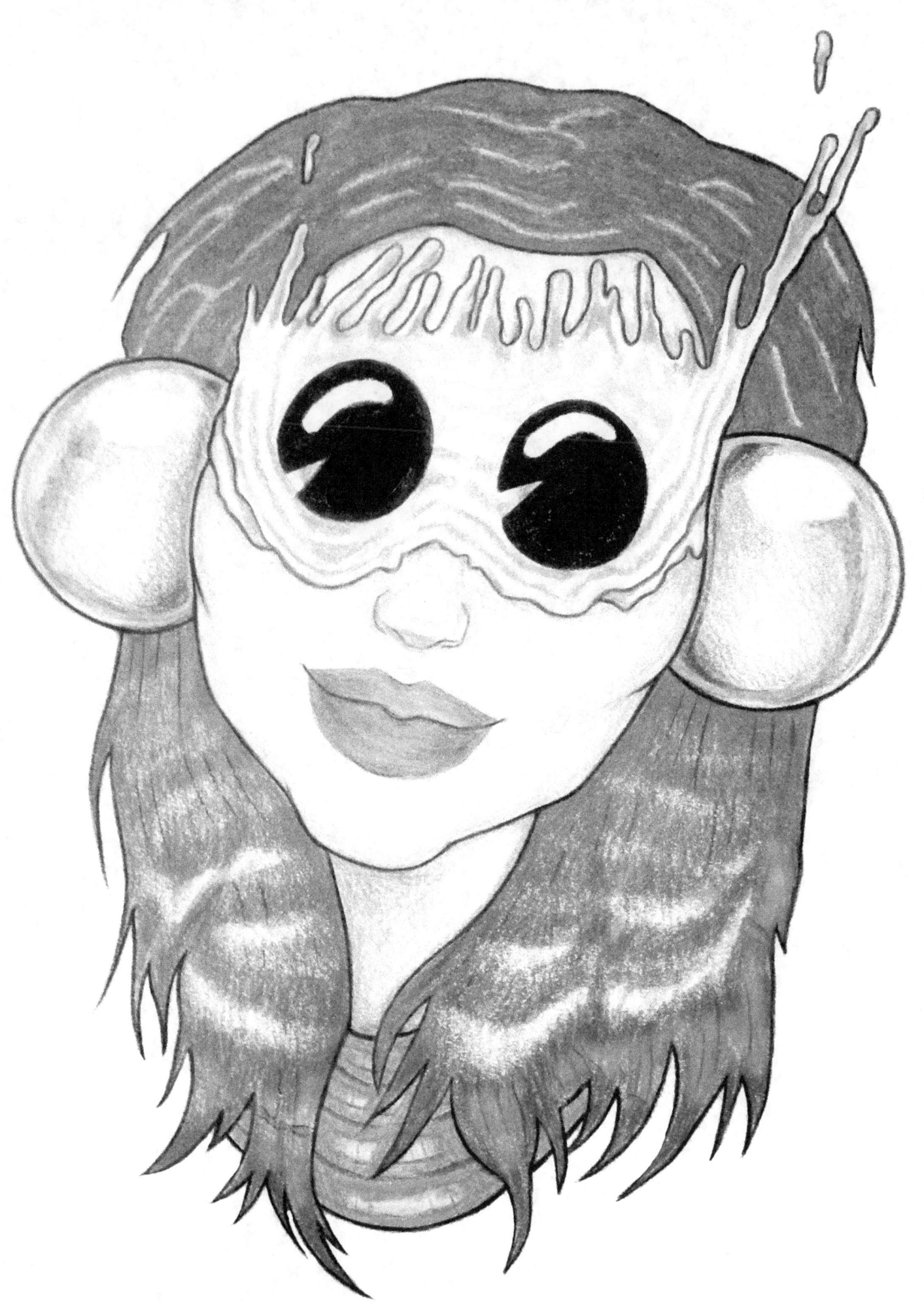

# Melty Meteor

Age: 20 Meteors Old
Location: Hurtling through space at high speeds.
She loves scrambled eggs.

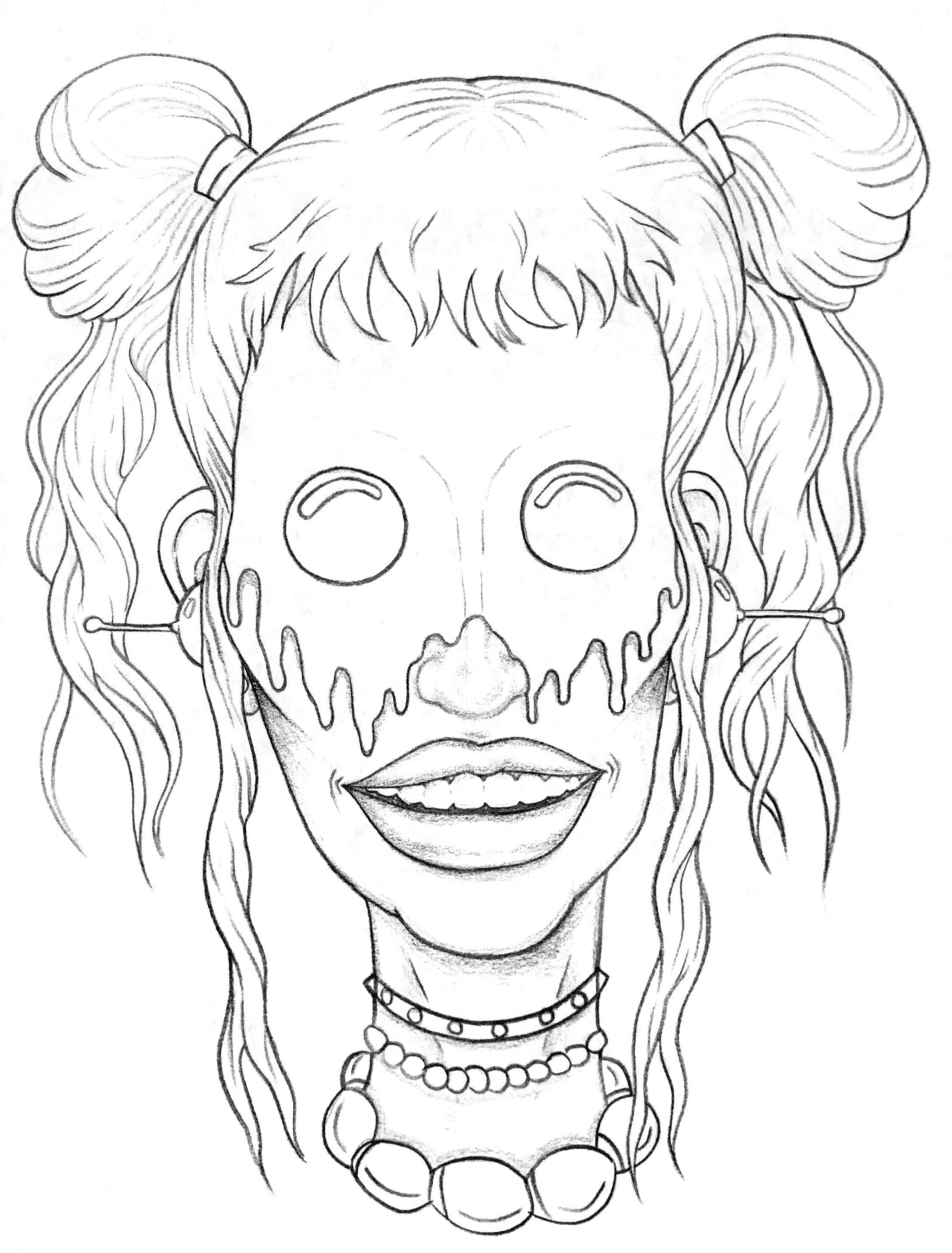

# Atomic Ashley

Age: 108 Robot Years
Location: Currently living on the Planet of Storms.
She loves a rainy day.

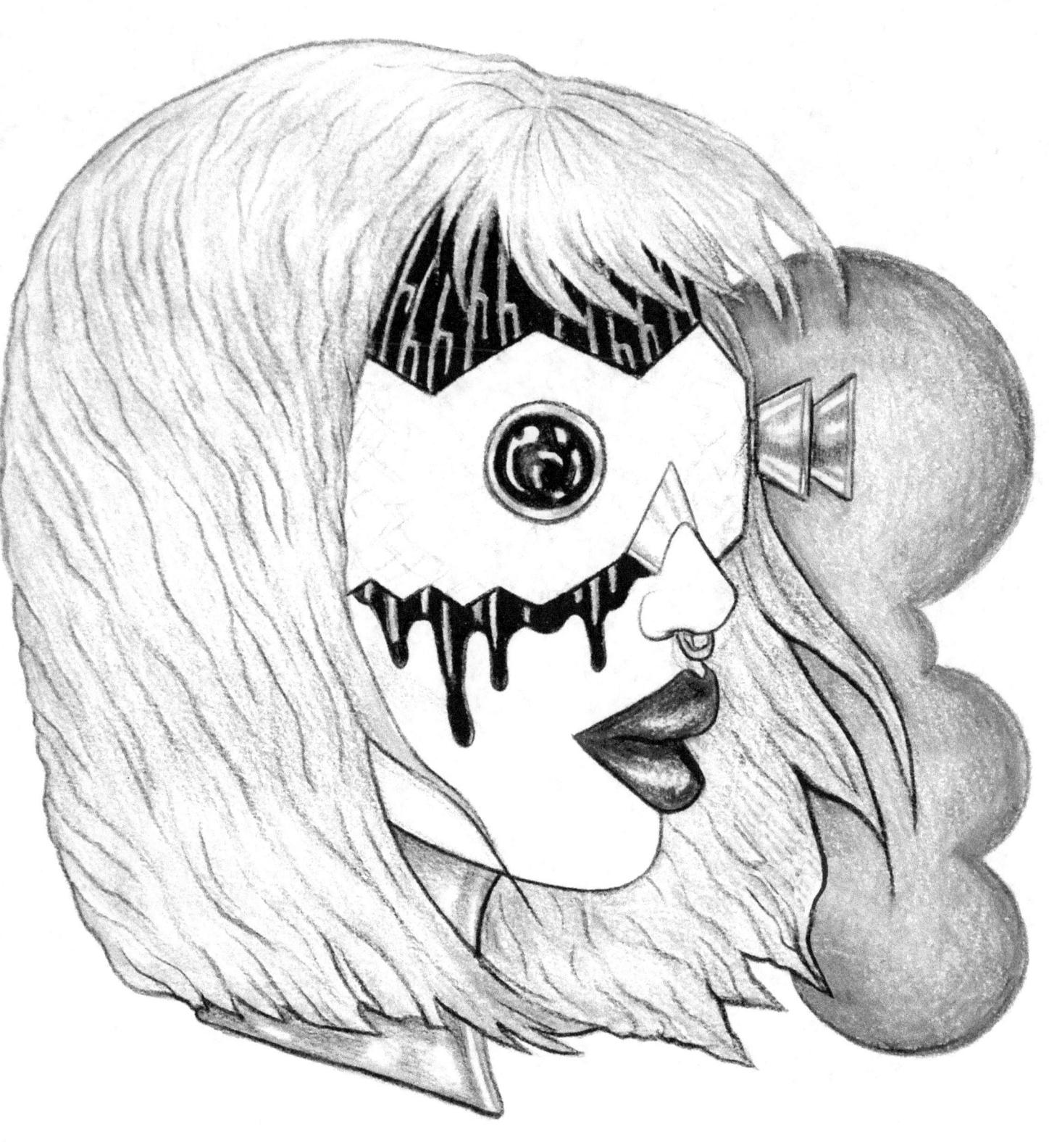

# Lucy Laser

Age: 19 Earth Years
Location: Currently living on campus at Space
University.
She only sleeps one hour a day.

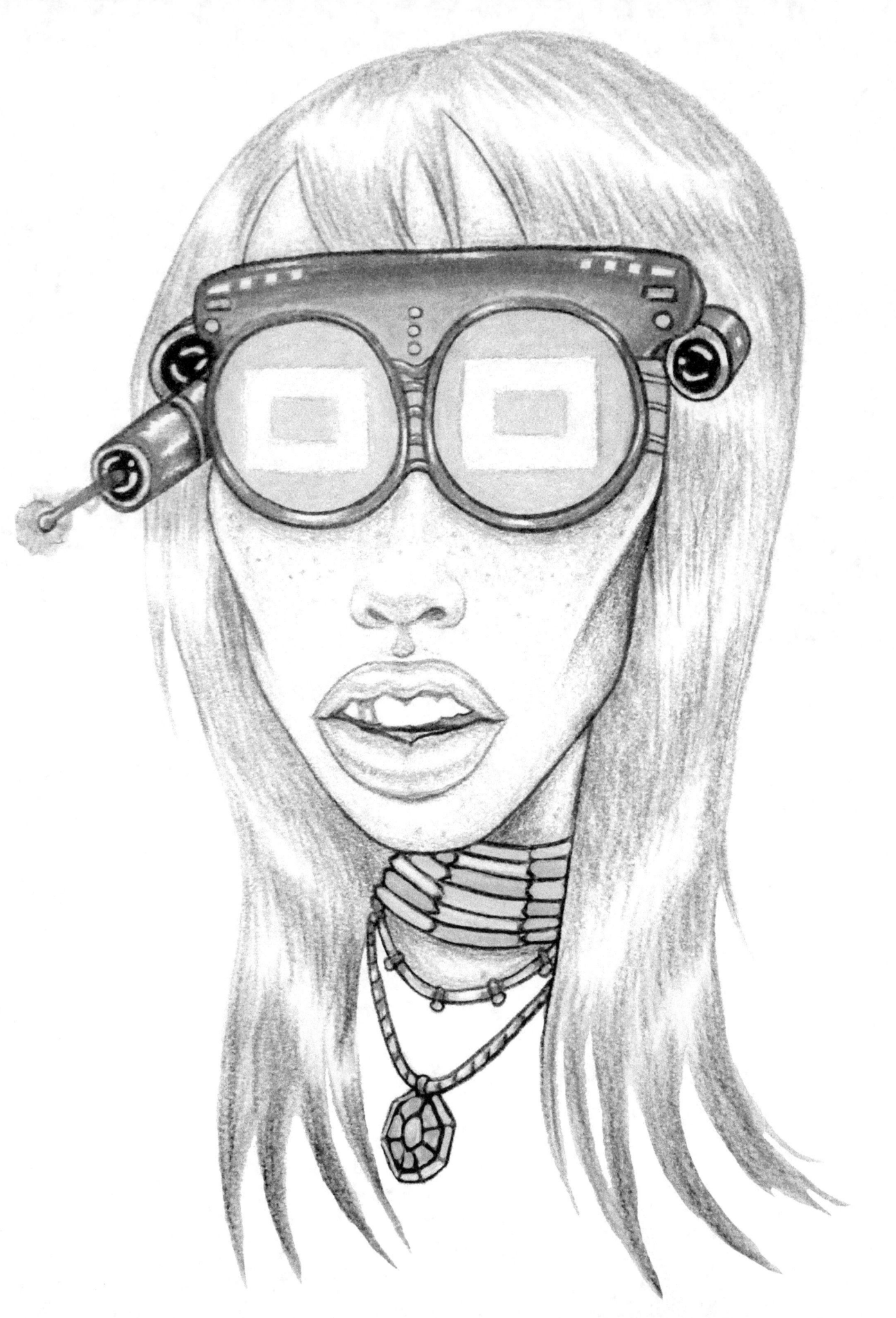

# Melissa Moondust

Age: 27 Melissa Years
Location: Currently living on Planet Melissa.
She is the Queen of her planet!

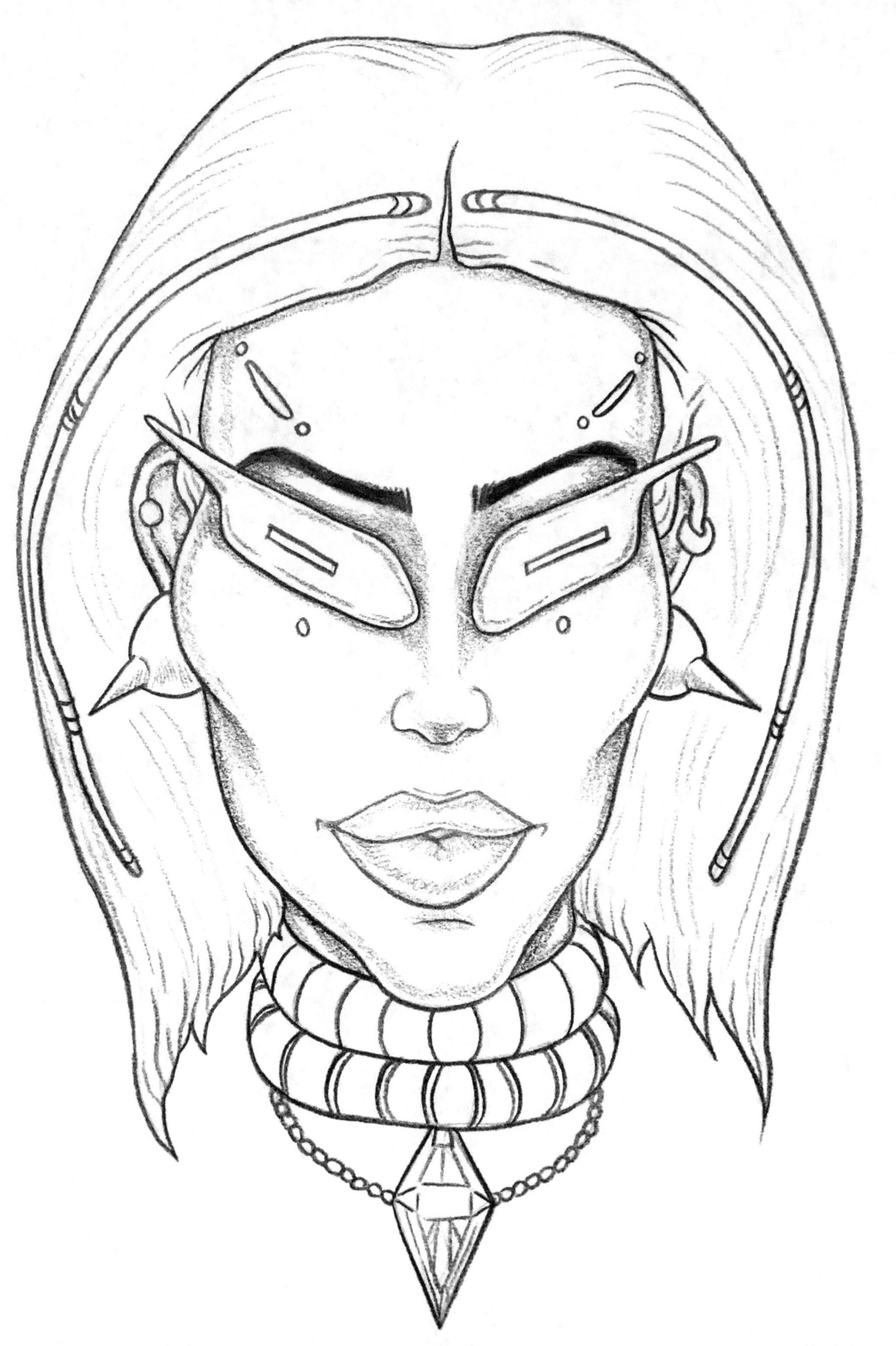

# Toni Taurus

Age: 23 Earth Years
Location: Currently working on Casino Planet.
She is a celebrated space go-go dancer.

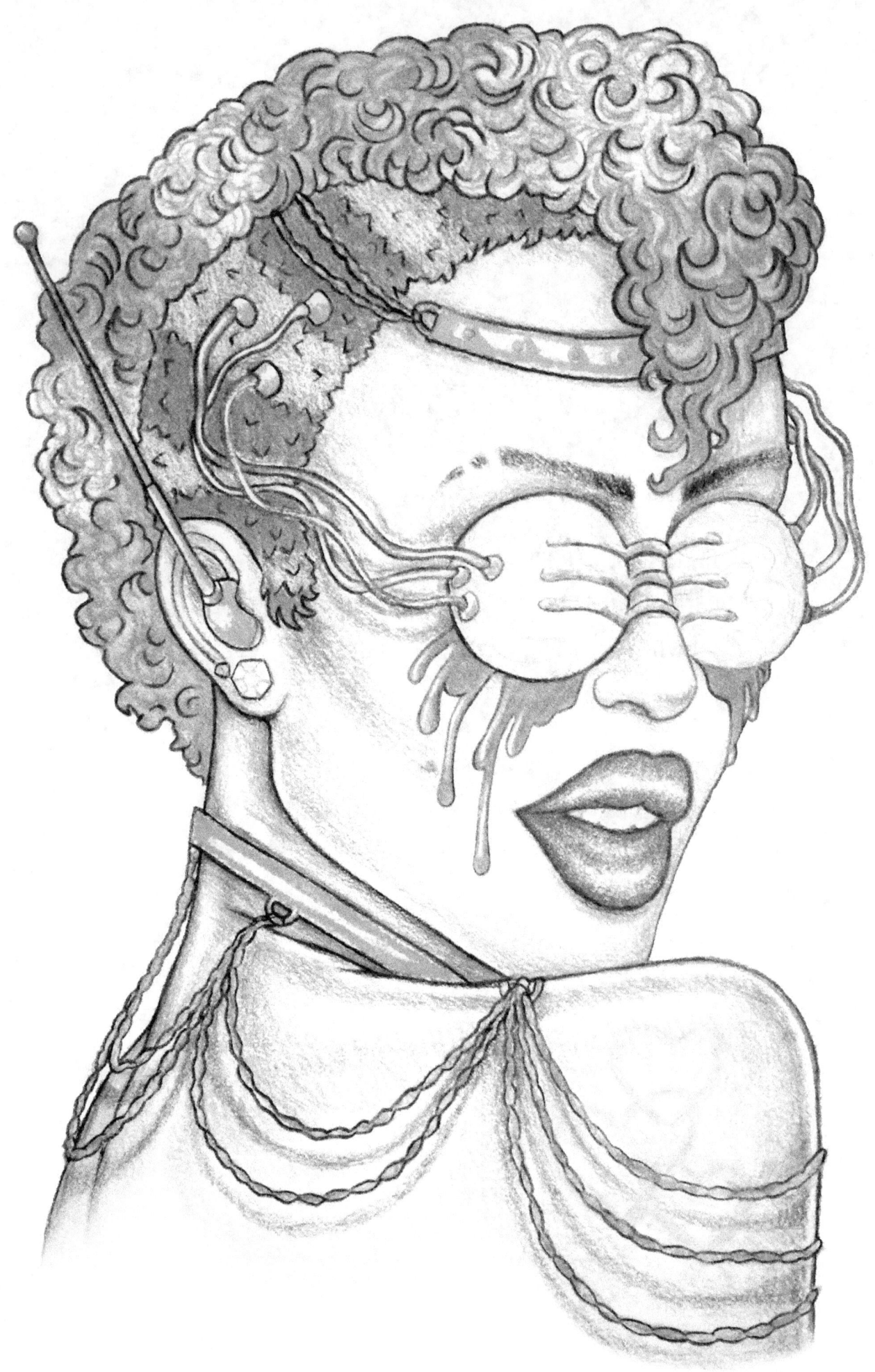

# Betty Blastoff

Age: 35 Earth Years
Location: Currently lives in the Shopping District.
She owns a clothing store in a space mall.

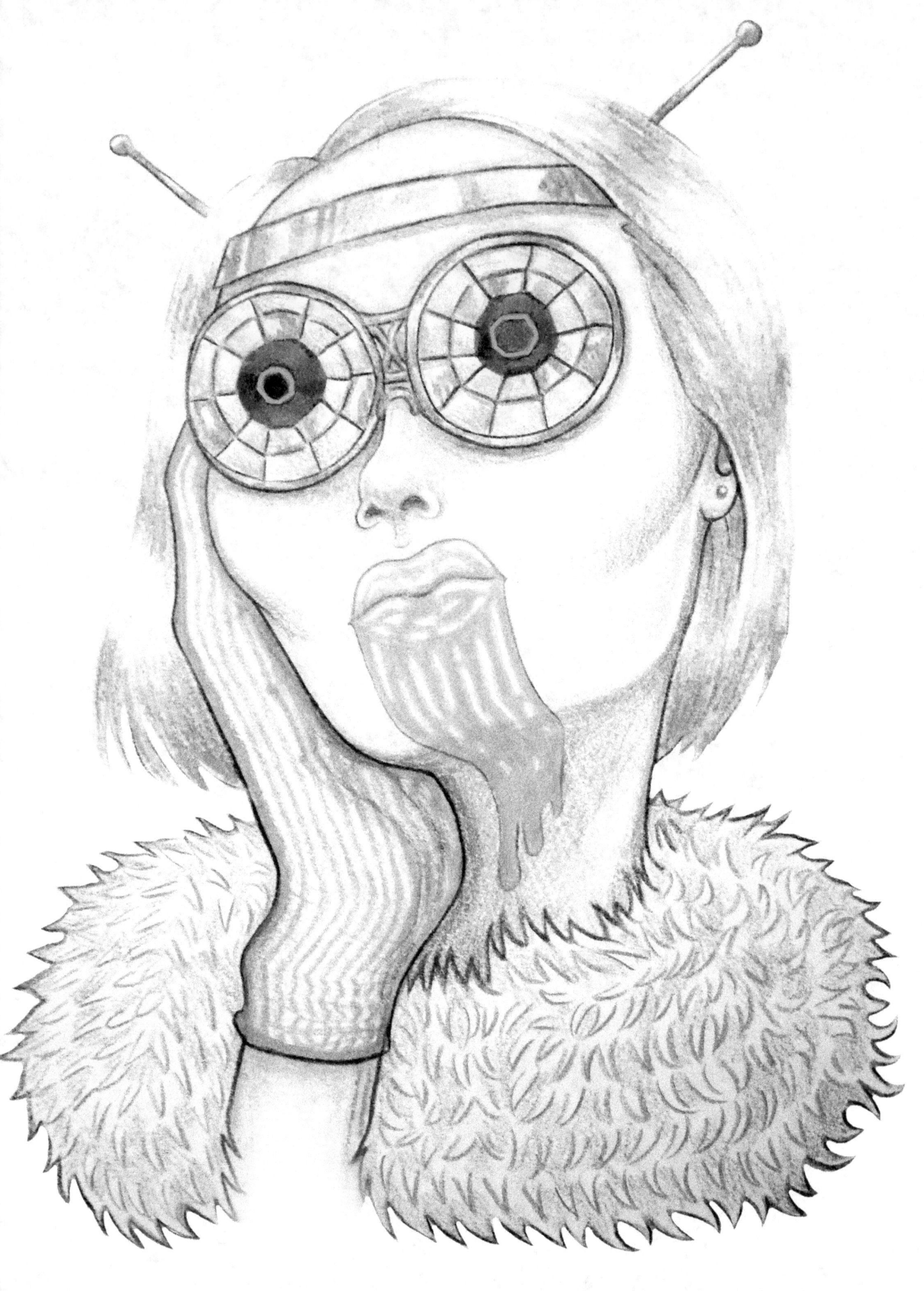

# Sandra Solarstorm

Age: 21 Earth Years
Location: A party near you!
She is currently studying accounting.

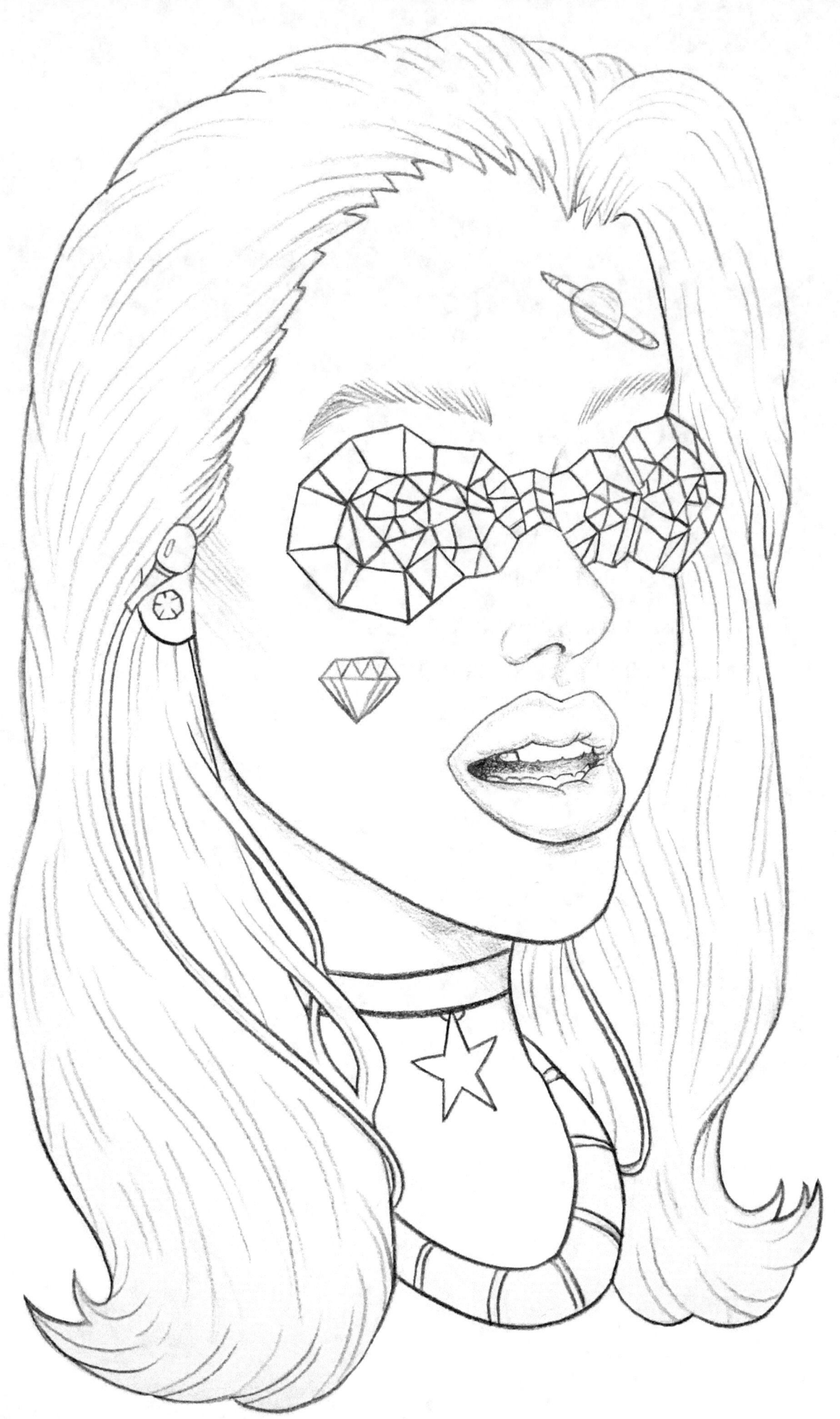

# Vivian Void

Age: 21 Earth Years
Location: Looking for trouble!
She is a famous space criminal.

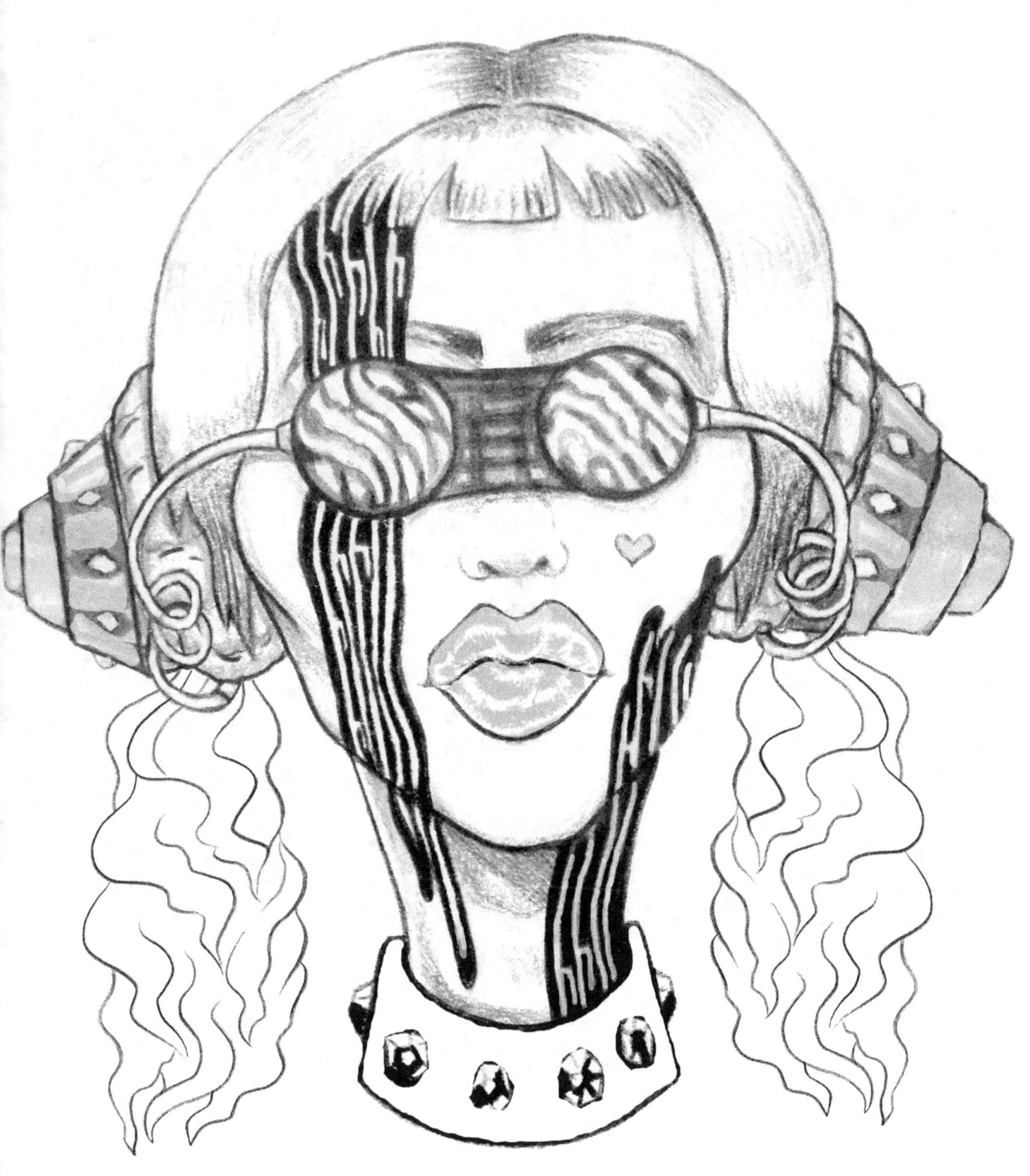

# Suzie Squirrel

Age: 3 Squirrel Years
Location: Currently living in a tree.
Both of her parents are squirrels!

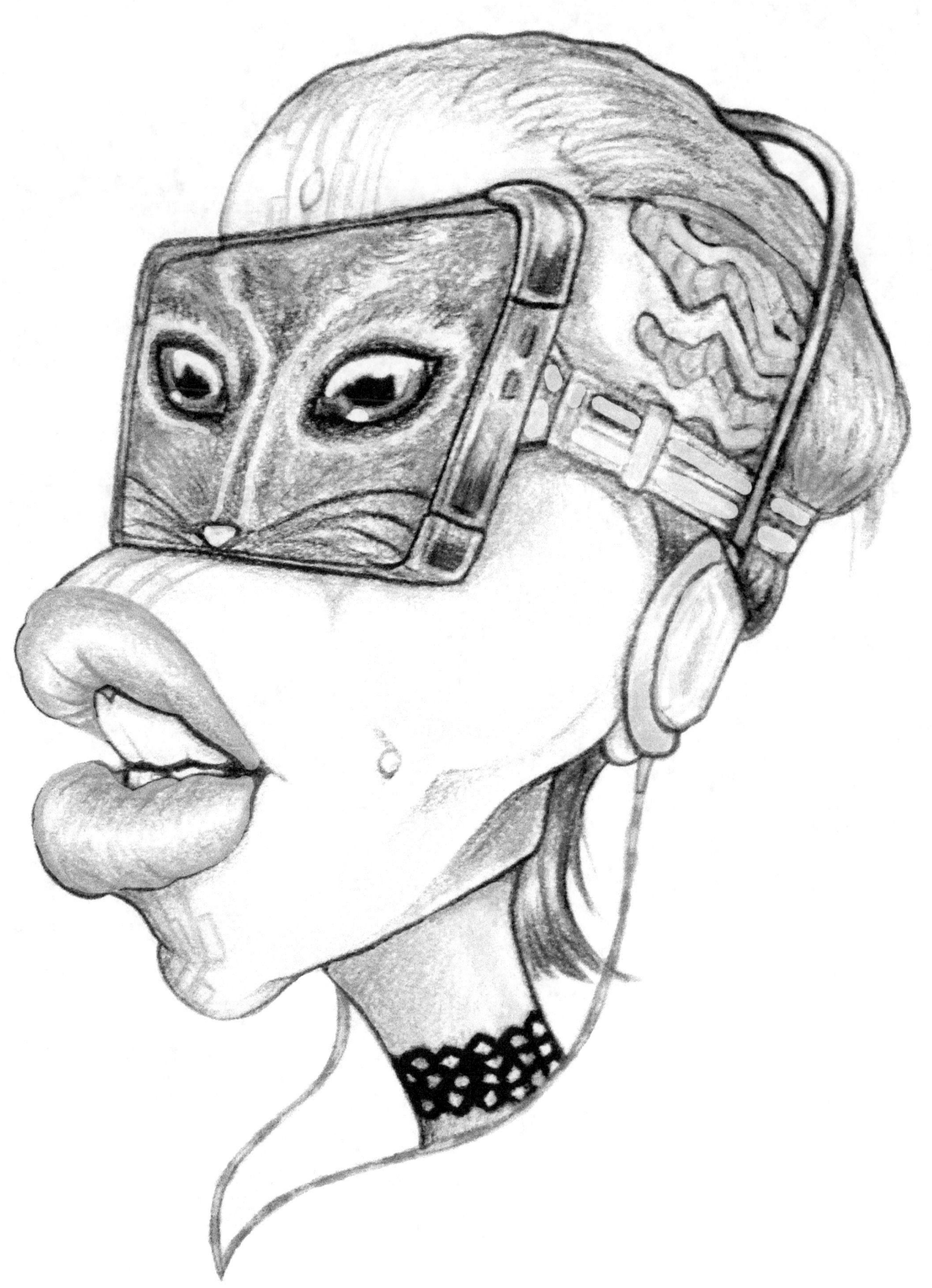

# Selena Star

Age: 22 Star Years
Location: Currently living on the North Star.
She is a Star Princess.

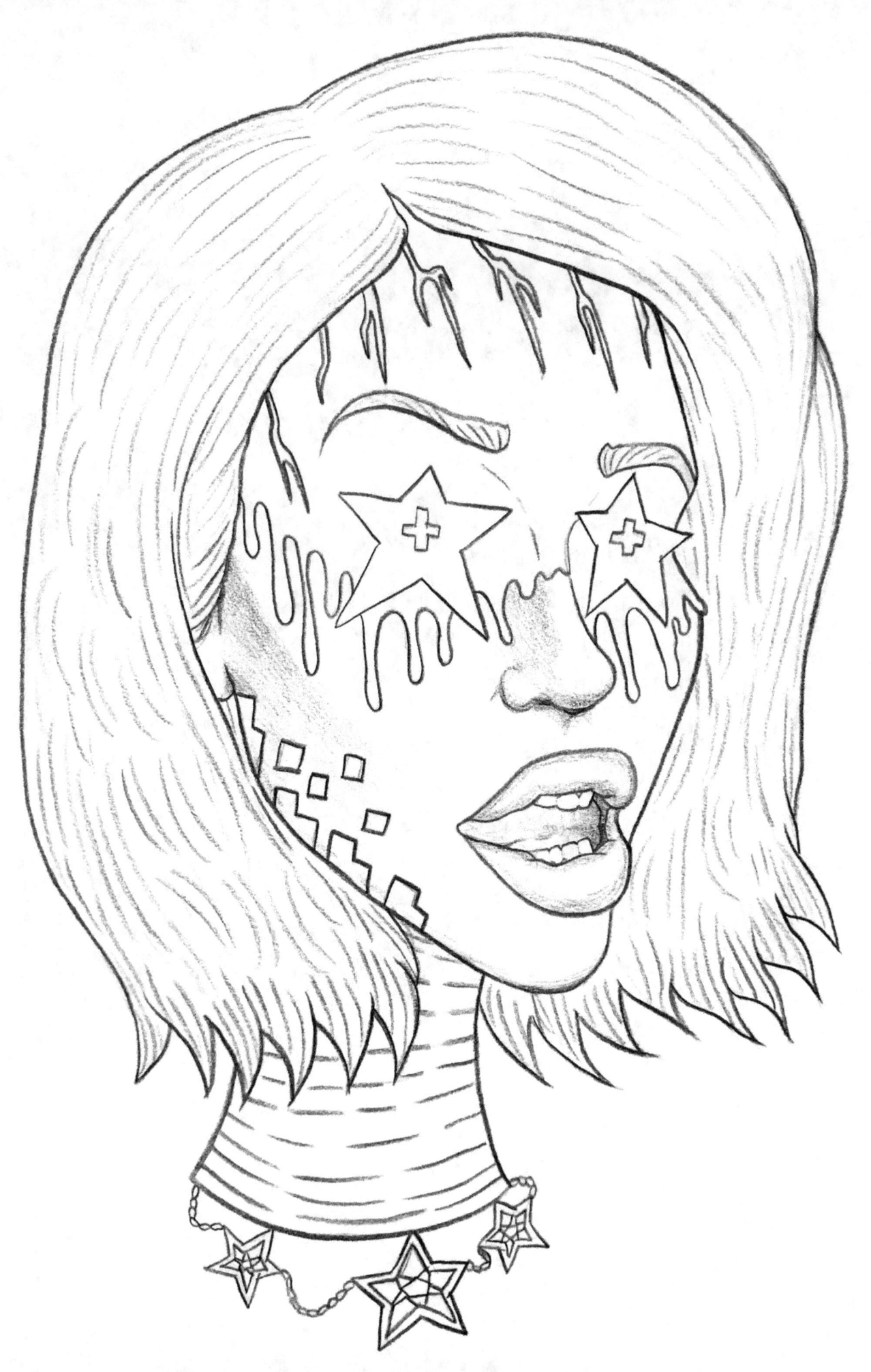

# Sharon Sugar

Age: 29 Earth Years
Location: Currently living on the Ice Cream
Planet.
She has a lot of dogs.

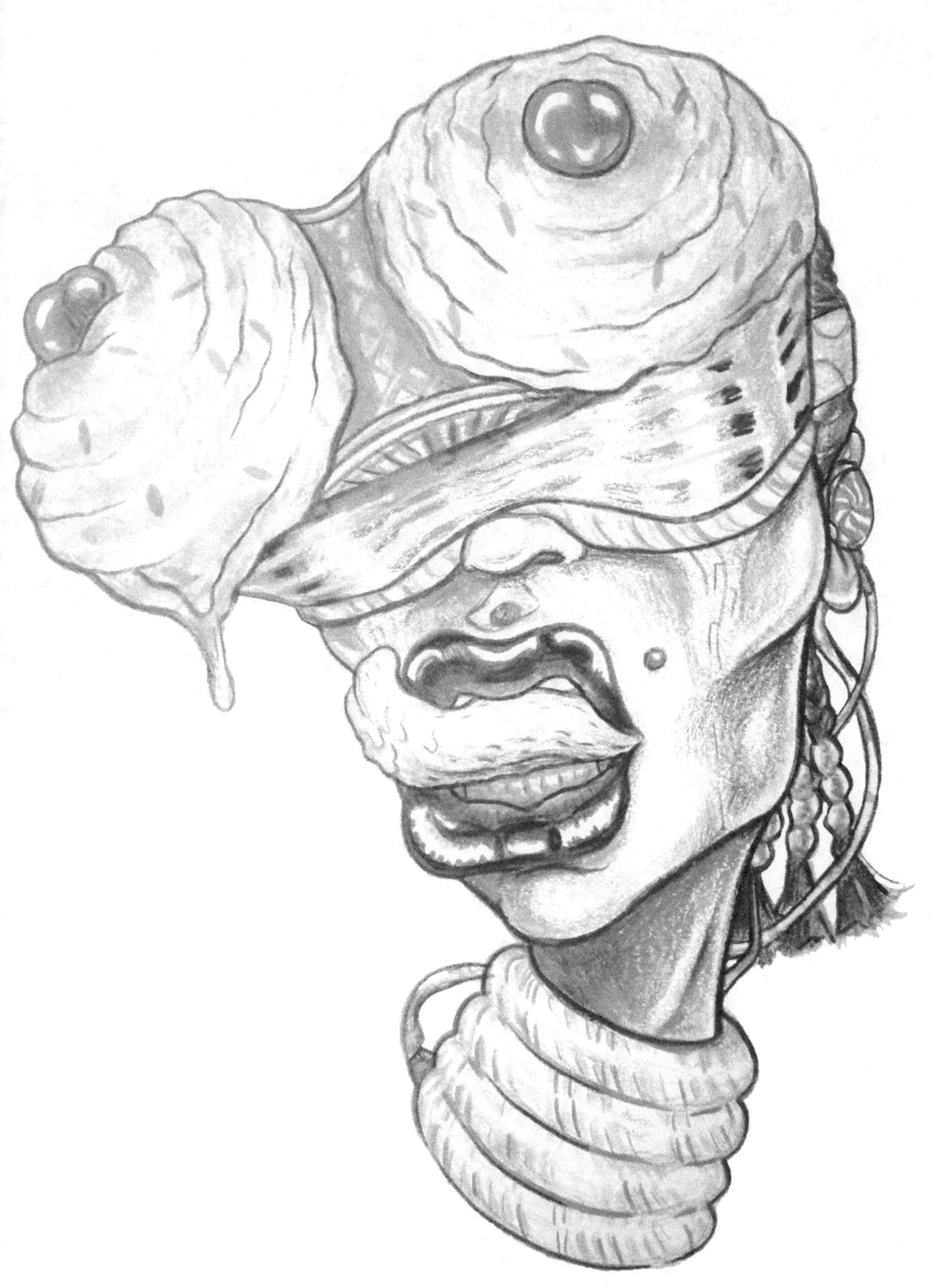

# Cindy Circuit

Age: 24 Computer Years
Location: Currently living in a computer.
Don't look into her eyes!

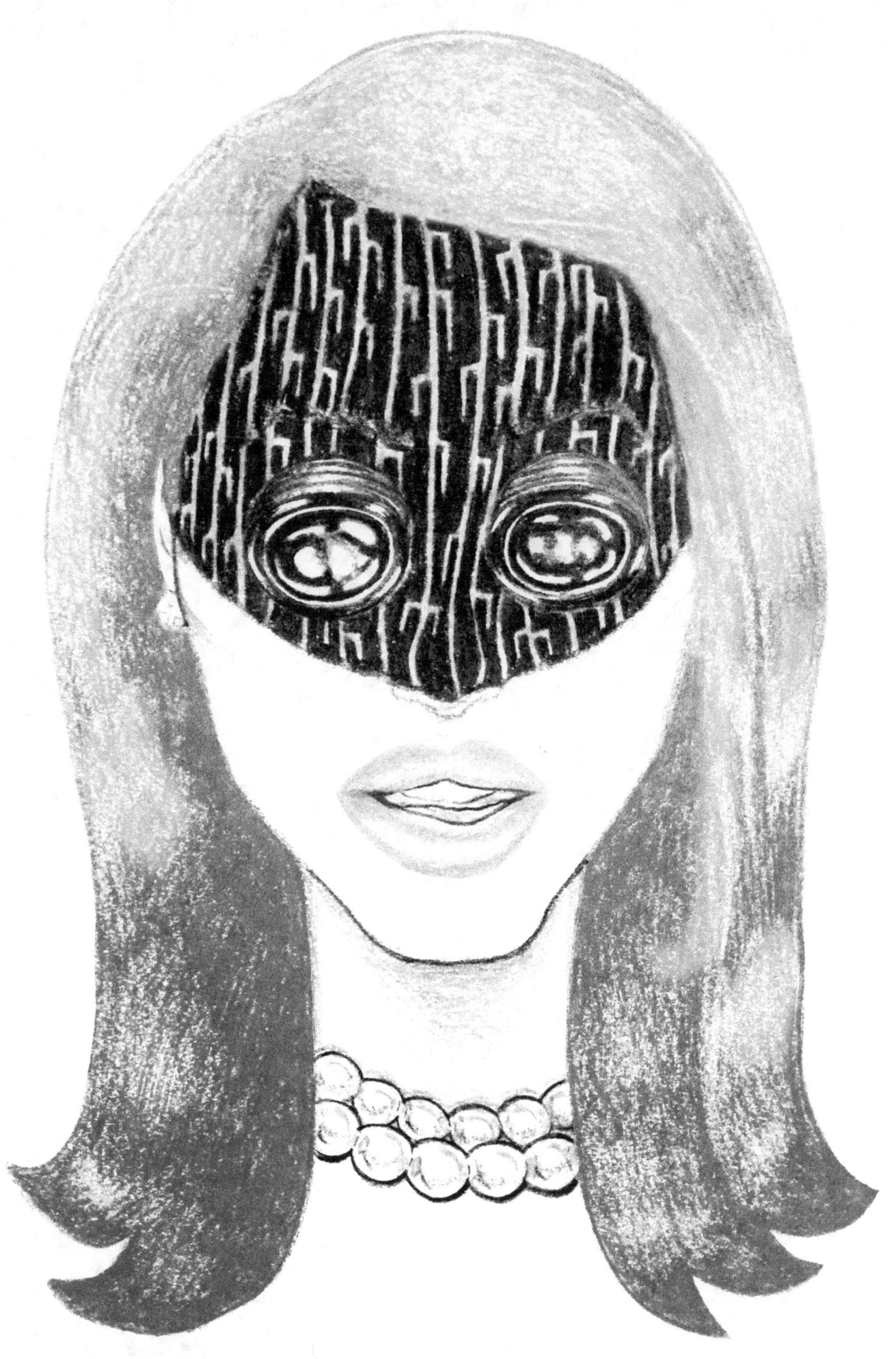

# Ellen Eclipse

Age: 200 Space Years
Location: Currently living on the Moon.
She loves road trips!

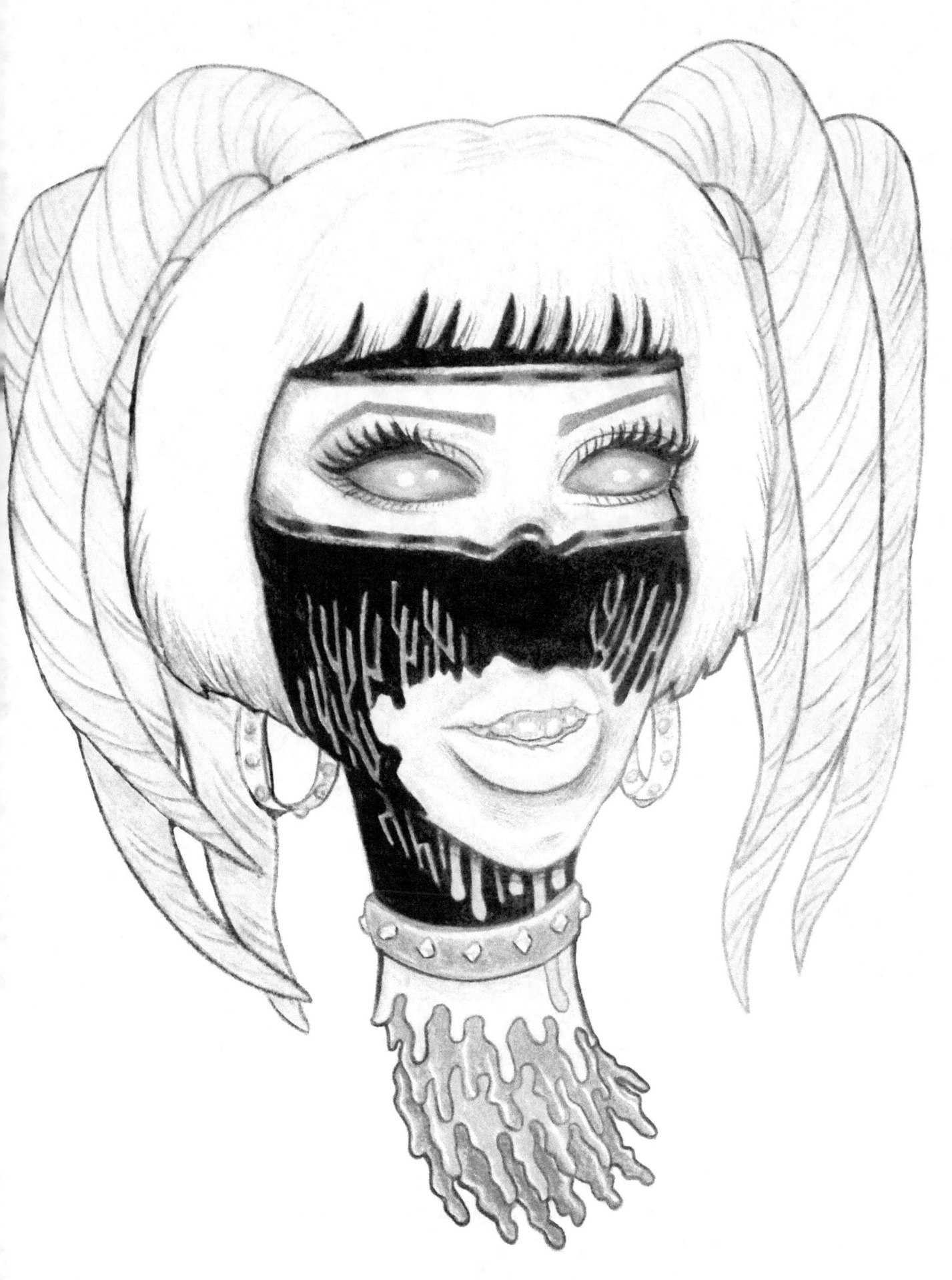

# Sammie Cyborg

Age: 1200 Computer Years
Location: Currently living in the Ancient Space
Library.
She loves to sing!

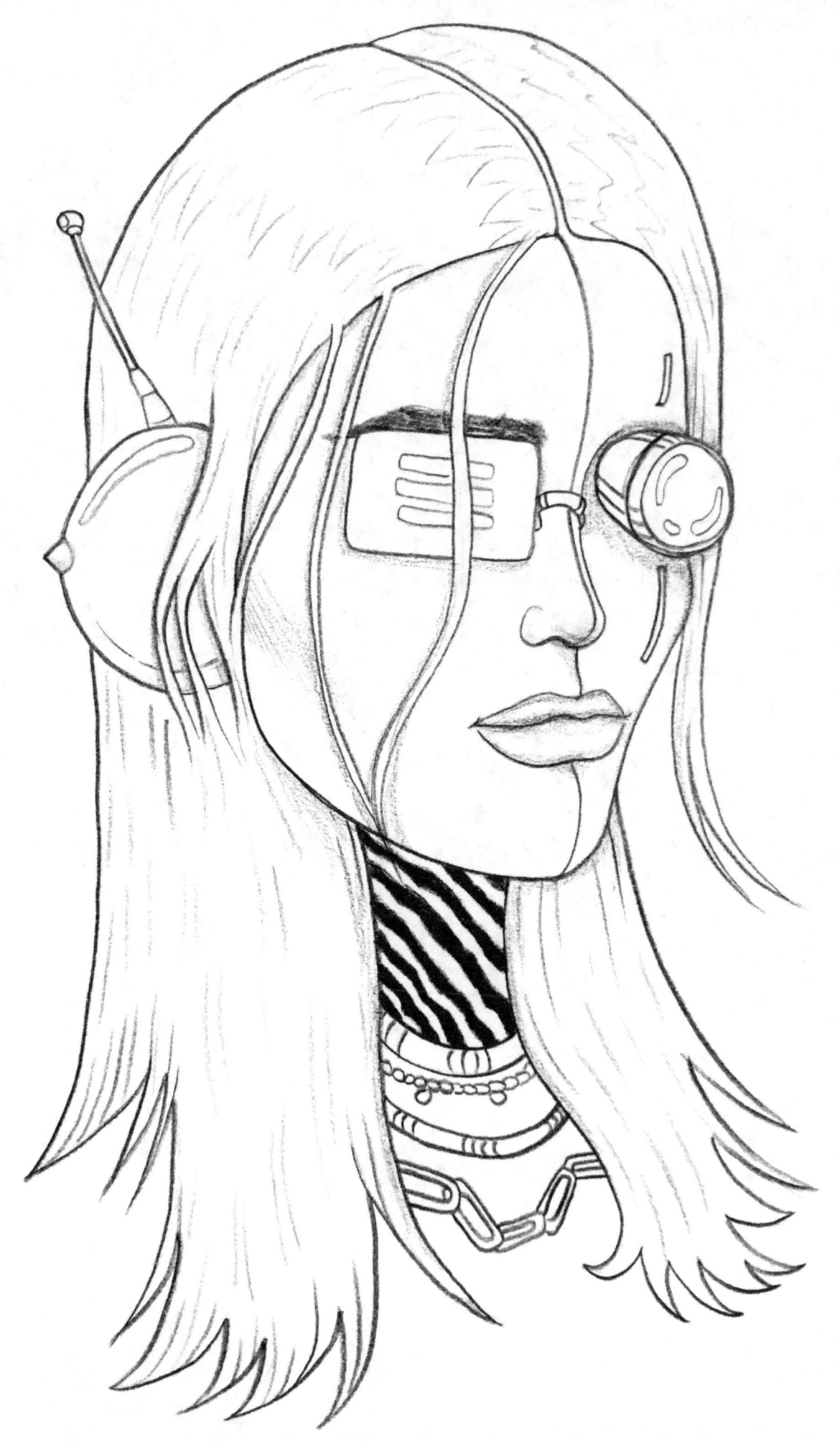

# Debbie Download

Age: 18 Earth Years
Location: Currently living on Jupiter.
She enjoys all sports.

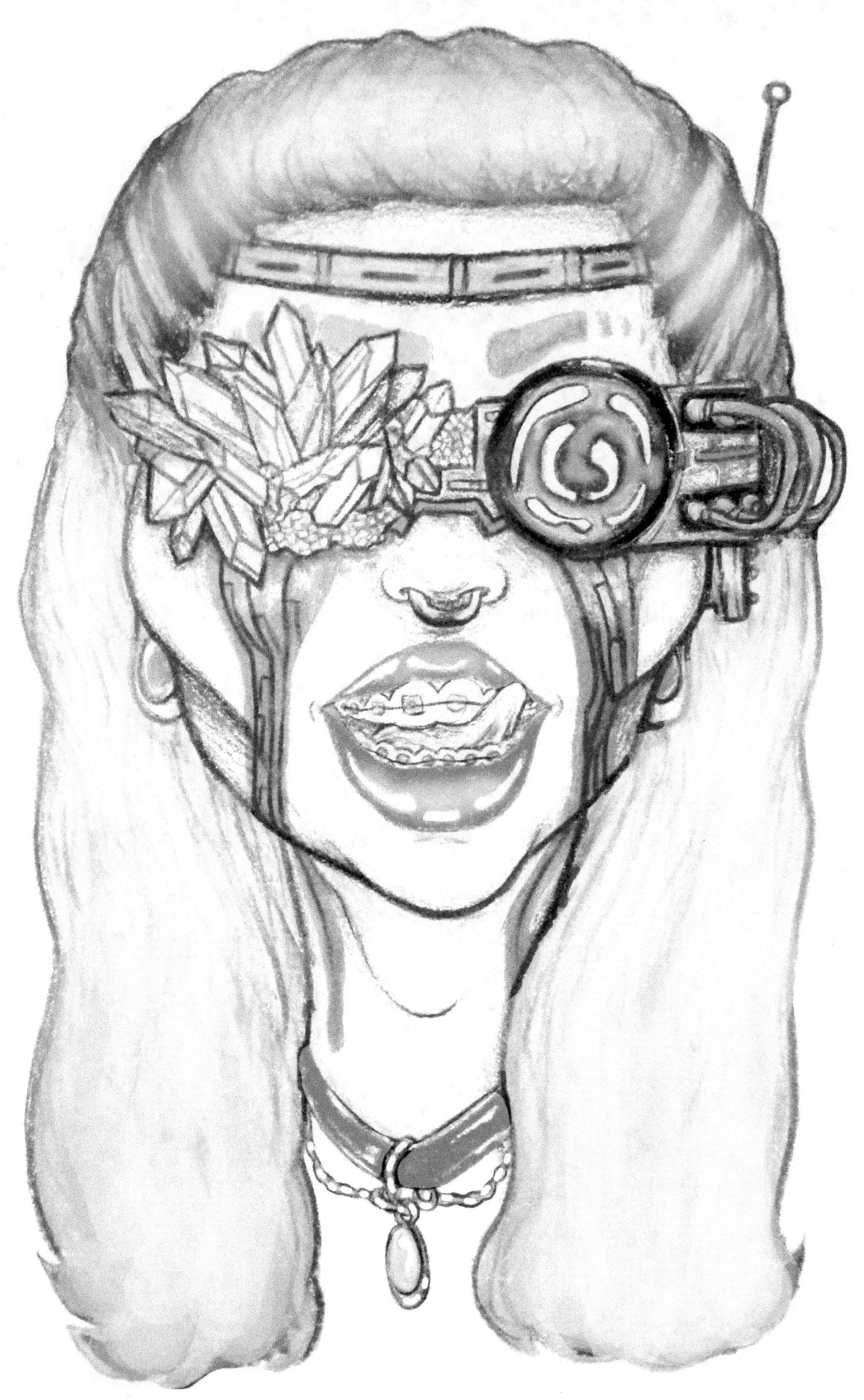

# Beanie Girl

Age: 23 Earth Years
Location: Currently lives on the edge of the Solar System.
She is a champion surfer.

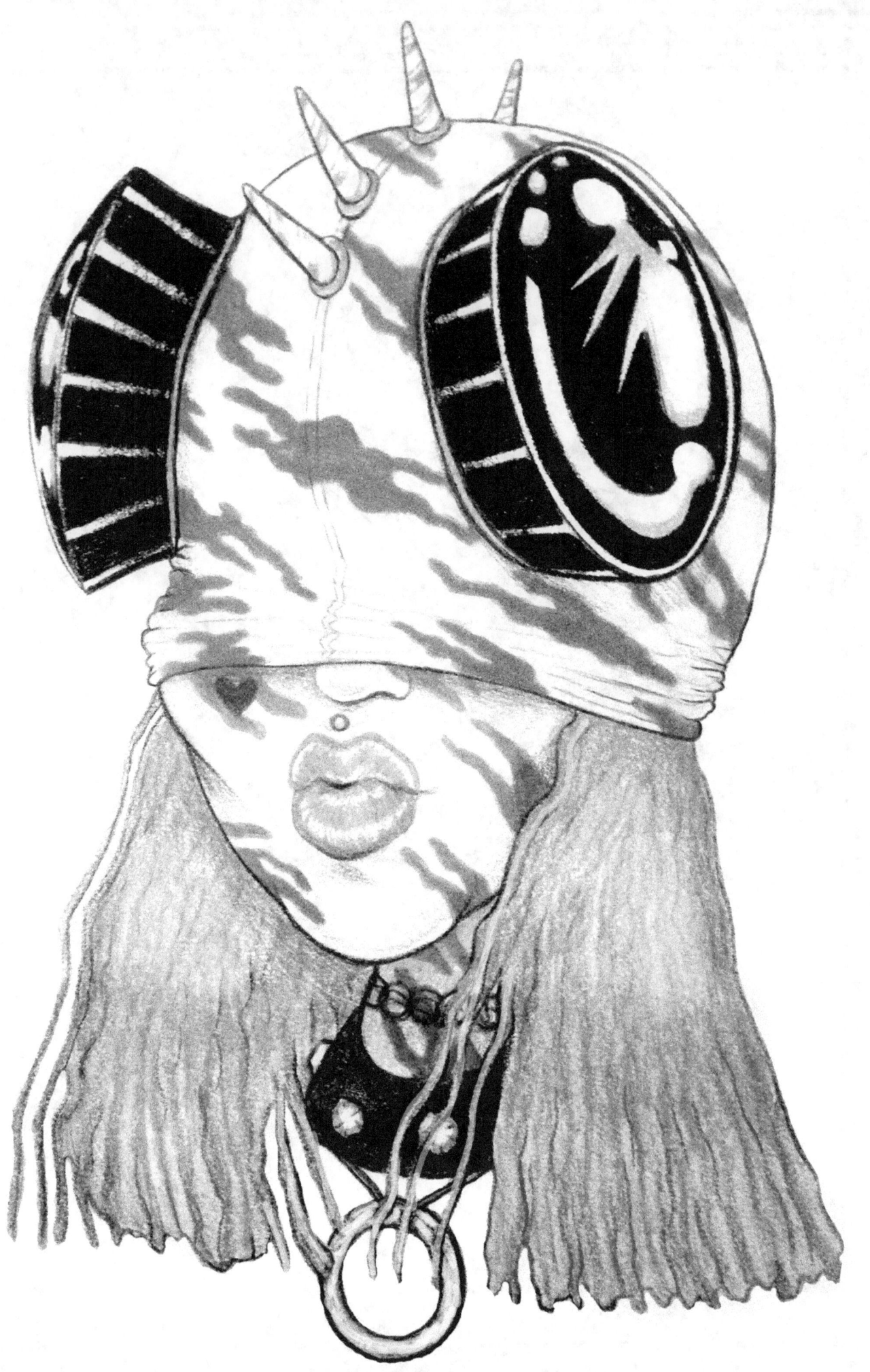

# QC
## Quinn Collectibles
## Coloring Books!
### By Stephanie A. Quinn

# Art For Everyone!

Here at Quinn Collectibles, we believe in Art For Everyone!

**No Pressure** - You don't have to be Michelangelo to enjoy a relaxing session of coloring. Now is the time to let your imagination run wild and put some blue lipstick on that golden retriever!

**Experimentation** - Finished coloring your page and notice that you have some space leftover? Why not draw a flower of your own and color it in!

**Fun** - If you're not having fun, what are you doing? Life is short, grab a box of your favorite crayons and get funky!

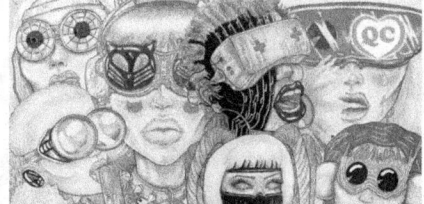 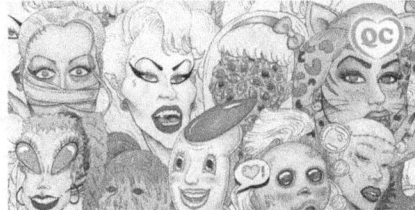 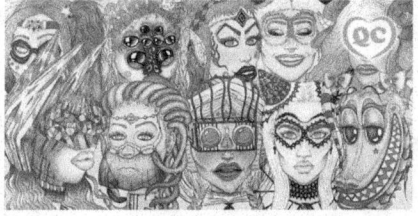
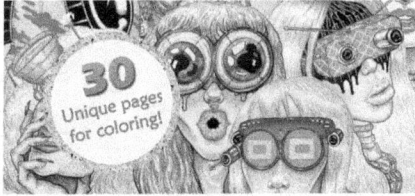 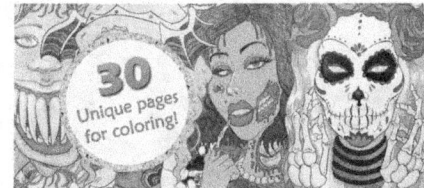 

www.ingramcontent.com/pod-product-compliance
Lightning Source LLC
Chambersburg PA
CBHW081254180526
45170CB00007B/2424

* 9 7 8 1 5 3 9 6 3 2 0 8 5 *